EDNA ST. VINCENT MILLAY

A Bibliography
of the Works of
EDNA ST. VINCENT MILLAY

BY

KARL YOST

With an Essay in Appreciation

BY

HAROLD LEWIS COOK

Introductions and Three Poems

BY

EDNA ST. VINCENT MILLAY

BURT FRANKLIN BIBLIOGRAPHY AND REFERENCE SERIES #149

BURT FRANKLIN
NEW YORK

Published By
BURT FRANKLIN
235 East 44th St.
New York, N.Y. 10017

ORIGINALLY PUBLISHED
NEW YORK: 1937
Reprinted 1968

Printed in U.S.A.

Contents

[v]

Contents

[vi]

Contents

EDNA ST. VINCENT MILLAY

AN ESSAY BY

Harold Lewis Cook

FOREWORD TO THE ESSAY

As to Mr. Cook's estimate of the quality of my work considered as poetry, even were I in a position to judge, I should not, obviously, be in a position to speak. But I have enjoyed reading this essay for several reasons which have nothing to do with that aspect of its subject, and one of these reasons I should like to state here.

It seems to me that Mr. Cook has an almost infallible understanding of my poetry considered as speech, that he knows not only what I am saying, but also under the impulsion of what sort of urge, what sort of temperamental and circumstantial exigency, I am saying it: in other words, he knows what the poem is about. I will give one example only, though I could give several.

It has sometimes astonished me that a writer in whose work the part played by death is seldom anything but that of Supreme Nuisance, an obstacle in the road of life, insurmountable and unskirtable, but lacking in majesty of outline and rather more infuriating than fearsome, should so often be spoken of as being engrossed with the subject of death. Let me take as an illustration, since Mr. Cook has dealt with this poem at some length in his essay, the opening poem in *The Buck in the Snow*, "Moriturus."

In a recently published compilation of American poetry, a well-known editor of anthologies writes of "Moriturus" that it "proceeds from an undignified fear" of death. I could cite no better instance of a thorough misconception. This is as if one should say of a small boy who, because it is his bed-time, is forcibly separated from a large plate of ice-cream, that he struggles and howls because he is afraid of his bed. Mr. Cook, as you will see in this essay, falls into no such error.

Nor does he fall into any other major error of interpretation. And, quite naturally, to the poet who both intends and expects his poetry to be comprehensible, it is gratifying to be assured that he has not said precisely the opposite of what he meant to say.

I take pleasure in writing this short appreciation of a thoughtful and lucid study of my work.

EDNA ST. VINCENT MILLAY

Steepletop
February, 1937

PREFACE

THE essay on Miss Millay's poetry contained in this volume makes no pretense to a final critical estimate of her work; at best one can do no more than approach a final evaluation of the talent of a contemporary. Miss Millay is at the height of her powers as a poet, her last volume representing a profoundly increased richness of poetic perception, expression, and subject matter. Her new poems, as yet unpublished, differ so startlingly in form and subject from their predecessors that at first glance they might well be the work of another poet. This being true, any critical conclusions to be drawn now would inevitably prove to be, if not false, at least inaccurate. In the following essay, therefore, I have attempted, very simply, to trace through successive volumes the growth of Miss Millay's work, in range and in artistry. It has been an enlightening study. That growth has been singularly the expression of a personal development and has remained unaffected by any literary movement of her time. It has brought Edna St. Vincent Millay to her present position as a lyric poet in the greatest tradition of English literature, and a sonneteer of the first order of genius.

These pages are a first step in the appreciation of that genius.

H. L. C.

EDNA ST. VINCENT MILLAY

I

IT IS evident to a reader of Miss Millay's work that she approaches poetry from its emotional side, treating her subject, even when it is intellectual, emotionally. It is equally evident that she seldom writes on a subject that has not moved *her* deeply—a qualification to be made only in speaking of the eminently sincere artist. This concern with the emotional aspect of her art—rather than the formal—indicates an intense poetic temperament. In spite of a superlative command of her medium, it is clear that Miss Millay is less interested in craftsmanship and its problems than she is in the intrinsic poetry of her subject. The point may be emphasized, for it is this love for, this concentration upon, the *poetry* that account for the lack of that experimentation so characteristic of many of her contemporaries. She has built her poems on ground that seemed to her permanent, rich, and deep, on fundamental and inexhaustible themes, on emotions, or ideas appreciated emotionally. One searches her books in vain for the latest psychology, the most recent attitude, the newest expression—in fact, for anything that is not as old as the hills and as new as the morning. A survey of her work shows no period disturbed by that preoccupation with formal experimentation so common among American poets of this generation (the men, particularly), and which so often indicates an uncertainty of direction or a

Edna St. Vincent Millay

weakness of poetic power which both exhausts and reveals itself in a nervous attempt at strength. It accounts, though perhaps less directly, for the fact that she is not read as a student and interpreter of the problems of her generation. Many of Miss Millay's contemporaries are already "historical," or rapidly becoming so. Their work will be valuable supplementary reading to a study of their period; their poems are brilliant commentaries on the ideas of economists, immigration bureaux, and social service commissions, on manners and morals, or they are brochures for a new school of writing. And in their categories they are important, for their work forms part of that great mass of second-rate poetry which, in the end, is most typical of any age, being, perhaps, a truer reflection of the spirit of that age than is the work (more detached and less prejudiced by the immediacy of social problems) of those few front-rank poets any given period may produce. Miss Millay's work, then, will never be read as history (except for the comment implied in the almost total absence of contemporaneous allusion), never be studied as invention (she writes in the most common and traditional forms of English verse), but will be read for its true accents of poetry, for its passion told in broad and simple lines that, in their sincerity, their unobtrusive rightness, are impressive.

To trace the development of Miss Millay's art is a revealing study. In the literary history of her time, so far as it concerns poetry, the year 1912 will be remembered for two events which have left their mark in a peculiarly stimulating fashion. Of these, the first—the founding by Harriet Monroe of *Poetry: A Magazine of Verse*—does not concern us here; the second, the publication in *The*

Edna St. Vincent Millay

Lyric Year of "Renascence," a poem written when the author was nineteen, introduced to the reading public a writer who has since become one of our most distinguished poets and who, almost alone among contemporary poets writing in America, has attained an international reputation. Since that date Miss Millay has published seven volumes of poetry and five of poetic plays, volumes which have given her a position permanent and unrivaled.

During the years since 1912, and particularly since 1914, American poetry has undergone many changes. Of the poets writing at the beginning of this period, who has survived? "In an age of revolutions in opinion, the co-temporary poets, those at least who deserve the name, those who have an individuality of character, if they are not before their age, are almost sure to be behind it," wrote John Stuart Mill. But in this period there were no poets who were before their age (as, for example, Blake was before his); there were many who were of it, who expressed the slightest fluctuations of its surface, and who died, valiantly enough, with it. A few ignored it, or watched and profited by it, assimilating this sun and storm, dispassionately, intelligently absorbing all, noting, as they note the changes in the sea, the restless variety of man. A few, looking on, maintained their own integrity, were little if at all influenced by the commotion of a period whose activities were frequently the result of hysteria, and whose literary productions were, on the whole, sensational, and frequently merely occasional. For these few, war, economic and social upheavals, theories, and movements were not of prime importance as subjects for poetry. Nature, love, and death; man amid the stars; man and God—these were subjects which seemed to them more

[9]

important and more moving. Hardy, in 1915, had made the point magnificently in "In Time of the Breaking of Nations," and it is interesting to note that I. A. Richards, one of the critics most concerned (and by means of the newest techniques) with the position and interpretation of poetry in our time, is forced to recommend as a kind of measuring-rod of great poetry five suggestions or frames into which it is easier to fit the poetry of Shakespeare and Miss Millay than that, say, of the Obscurantists or the Objectivists.

Miss Millay is one of the few present-day poets in America whose development as poets has been synonymous with their development as individuals. The literary movements of their day have affected them scarcely at all. They can write a poem (as Landor said of Wordsworth) without the aid of war. Their work shows little influence; what can be traced in it that is not strictly individual is common to English poetry since Chaucer. It is this fact, among others, that makes "Renascence" so astonishing a performance. Modern poets at the age of nineteen are rarely writing in an idiom so definitely personal, are rarely recording an experience so pre-eminently sincere; their emotions are derivative and literary, though they believe them to be their own. For a parallel to "Renascence" we must go back to the poets of the seventeenth century, to Herbert, Vaughan, and Crashaw, or earlier, to Southwell. These men record mystical experiences, but they are the calm, profoundly religious ecstasies of maturity. "Renascence" is a cry of amazed joy, of terror and delight, youthful, fresh, and untutored, one feels, by any religious or literary training whatsoever. It is unique among Miss Millay's poems, though echoes of the same feeling sound in

Edna St. Vincent Millay

"God's World," and, somewhat diminished, in "The Blue-Flag in the Bog." The poem itself and its chronological position in Miss Millay's work provide a striking example of Wordsworth's "vision splendid"; one "perceives it die away" as the poet grows older, and finally "fade into the light of common day." This special "vision" fades and the accompanying ecstasy becomes less and less poignant, but the love of nature which inspired it and the passion which carried its crescendo movement to a climax remain to supply homely or noble background and emotion to later work.

One marvels again and again at the extraordinary spontaneity of the poem; it would be difficult indeed to trace any line in it to a source outside the poet's own personality. Even more inexplicable is the sudden appearance of this poem in the work of a young girl whose published poetry had been confined to the pages of *St. Nicholas Magazine* and her high-school paper, *The Megunticook*. Miss Millay "graduated" from the *St. Nicholas* League in 1910, when she was eighteen years old. Her first contribution, to the number of October, 1906, had been a piece called "Forest Trees," which opened with the resounding lines (she was fourteen),

> Monarchs of long-forgotten realms, ye stand;
> Majestic, grand;
> Unscarred by Time's destructive hand.
>
> Enthroned on dais of velvet moss, inset
> With the royal purple of the violet;

This had been followed over a period of four years by verses bearing such titles as "The Land of Romance," "After the Celebration (as told by the Firecracker)," "Va-

Edna St. Vincent Millay

cation Song," "Life," "Day's Rest Time," "Young Mother Hubbard," and finally by "Friends," which won for its author a cash prize and was her valedictory.[1] The benefits she derived from her association with *St. Nicholas* she recorded in a letter published in the issue of October, 1910:

CAMDEN, ME.

DEAR ST. NICHOLAS:

I am writing to thank you for my cash prize and to say good-by, for "Friends" was my last contribution. I am going to buy with my five dollars a beautiful copy of "Browning," whom I admire so much that my prize will give me more pleasure in that form than in any other.

Although I shall never write for the League again, I shall not allow myself to become a stranger to it. You have been a great help and a great encouragement to me, and I am sorry to grow up and leave you.

Your loving graduate,

EDNA VINCENT MILLAY

A few months after the above letter was written, Miss Millay wrote most of "Renascence." It was finished in the next year, and published in *The Lyric Year* in 1912. Here was a change indeed! Miss Millay, "sorry" or not, had "grown up." A poet had been born who was strong in her own right, whose harvest of knowledge was to be of her own sowing and reaping; whose house of words was strengthened by no timber not her own, the light to shine from its many windows the bright illumination of a spirit simple and honest and courageous. The house has mellowed with the years; its timbers have now weathered and toughened and its bright colors have deepened; its decora-

[1] See Appendix A.

tions, never extravagant, have become almost austere; its rooms are marvelously suited to their guests.

Miss Millay's first volume of verse appeared in 1917, under the title *Renascence*. Aside from its title poem, the volume contained twenty-two poems, of which some fifteen had been published in magazines. The title poem was already well known, and the reader could now speculate with interest on the probable magnitude of the author's talent. That first achievement was repeated in only one poem, "God's World," first printed in 1913. Here the fierce joy of her discovery of beauty had become a passionate violence; the spiritual quality of "Renascence" is missing. The remaining poems showed, in a striking fashion, what was happening to their author. She had not, for one thing, succumbed to the Free Verse and Imagist movements which were liberating some talents and paralyzing others. She was writing in the simplest of traditional forms. But her mood had changed: she was discovering the world of sorrow, as she had already discovered the world of beauty, and by 1914 we have "Interim"[1] (actually written in the year that *Renascence* was written), for all its many weaknesses a moving account of a young and sensitive heart's first encounter with the shock of death. Impetuously she places the responsibility:

> How easily could God, if He so willed,
> Set back the world a little turn or two!
> Correct its griefs, and bring its joys again!

[1] This poem, and the later "Sonnets from an Ungrafted Tree," dealing with pictures of death, are the result of pure observation plus the poet's imaginative setting, the author having at the time of their composition no experience of loss. The point is worth noting, since these poems have often been mentioned as particularly vivid records of personal grief.

Edna St. Vincent Millay

Her grief, however, failed, at times, to find an altogether controlled expression, and we have such lines as these:

—What do I say?
God! God!—God pity me! Am I gone mad
That I should spit upon a rosary?

The ecstatic realization of the universe, so poignantly, so naïvely, sung in "Renascence," becomes, toward the end of "Interim," the horror of meaninglessness:

How often over me
Flashes this breathlessness of sudden sight
In which I see the universe unrolled
Before me like a scroll and read thereon
Chaos and Doom, where helpless planets whirl
Dizzily round and round and round and round,
Like tops across a table, gathering speed
With every spin, to waver on the edge
One instant—looking over—and the next
To shudder and lurch forward out of sight—

For this, even the one solace is denied:

Would to God
I too might feel that frenzied faith whose touch
Makes temporal the most enduring grief;

and the poem concludes:

Ah, I am worn out—I am wearied out—
It is too much—I am but flesh and blood,
And I must sleep.

The despair of "Interim" leads to the fantasy of "The Suicide." The speaker curses Life, its sneers, its blows, its "glutted lash," for

In me all's sunk that leapt, and all that dreamed
Is wakeful for alarm,—

[14]

Edna St. Vincent Millay

and what was expected, but
not granted, in life had been so little:

> I asked of thee no favor save this one:
> That thou wouldst leave me playing in the sun!

The act of suicide brings him back again to God's house,
which—for all its beauty—palls, there being no task in-
trusted to this newcomer to perform, though all about him
the "serene, grave servants go." At last he begs of God
some

> little task
> To dignify my days.—
> "Child," my father's voice replied,
> "All things thy fancy hath desired of me
> Thou hast received. . . .
> But as for tasks—" he smiled and shook his head;
> "Thou hadst thy task and laidst it by," he said.

This reproof, gentle though it be, is the solitary example
in Miss Millay's poetry of heavenly rewards and punish-
ments. What Heaven or what Hell we are to know, we
are henceforth to know on earth. And so, when we reach
"Ashes of Life" (not Miss Millay's title), the world has
become very small indeed, and Heaven is far away. The
horizon has narrowed to the circle of daily existence:

> . . . life goes on forever like the gnawing of a mouse,—
> And tomorrow and tomorrow and tomorrow and tomorrow
> There's this little street and this little house.

The volume concludes with six sonnets, the form in
which has been cast the poetry that has brought Miss Millay her greatest fame, among them "Time does not bring
relief," her first published sonnet. Already the poet seems
at home in this most exacting poetic form; its demands
have exerted a needed discipline, and the looser and fre-

Edna St. Vincent Millay

quently too facile statement characteristic of some of the other poems in this volume is now molded to a deeper and more concentrated expression. With this concentration of form has come a necessary intensification of thought and emotion. The delicate impatience, the over-dramatic cry does not adapt itself readily to the richer, more contrapuntal harmonies of the sonnet. Words must be weighed; the pace is slower; each phrase must have its own value; but the unity of the whole cannot for a moment be sacrificed. The discipline has proved fruitful, and since *Renascence* each successive volume of Miss Millay's work has produced increasingly fine sonnets, until, in *Fatal Interview*, and "Epitaph for the Race of Man," we have sequences which demand comparison with that of Shakespeare.

The final statement of the descending note which prevails through the volume, we get in the sestet of Sonnet iv:

> So is no warmth for me at any fire
> To-day, when the world's fire has burned so low;
> I kneel, spending my breath in vain desire,
> At that cold hearth which one time roared so strong,
> And straighten back in weariness, and long
> To gather up my little gods and go.

Where she was to go almost inevitably—being young, and hurt—was to the defiant, sometimes pathetic, gaiety of her next volume, *A Few Figs From Thistles.*

These poems, appearing first in 1920 as an issue of *Salvo*, and reprinted with additions in 1921, have been heartily abused by some critics, and somewhat over-praised by others; they have shocked, and they have delighted. Their author was accused of being a pagan, of being a nun, of being both at once; she had no conscience at all, or so much that it was constantly pursuing her; she was disgrac-

Edna St. Vincent Millay

ing her talent, or she was exposing a new, light, and amusing aspect of it. What the book really did was to prove that Miss Millay was a very normal young person who, having been disappointed and exasperated, was having a quite giddy little fling in the face of her foe. Insufficient money, a heady life in Greenwich Village after a somewhat troublous graduation from Vassar, a very keen sense of humor, and a youthful delight in her own virtuosity— all these combined to produce from the thistles of her daily existence these winy little figs:

> Was it for this I uttered prayers,
> And sobbed and cursed and kicked the stairs,
> That now, domestic as a plate,
> I should retire at half-past eight?

she wails in "Grown-Up." What might be plucked from the day, she would take; *carpe diem* was one road to knowledge or escape. She states this with winning grace in "Daphne":

> Why do you follow me?—
> Any moment I can be
> Nothing but a laurel-tree.
>
> Any moment of the chase
> I can leave you in my place
> A pink bough for your embrace.
>
> Yet if over hill and hollow
> Still it is your will to follow,
> I am off!—to heel, Apollo!

But she was forced to admit, unwillingly as a stubborn child, that there were some compensations, frustrated though she be. In "The Prisoner" we can hear her stamp her foot as she cries:

[17]

Edna St. Vincent Millay

All right,
Go ahead!
What's in a name?
I guess I'll be locked into
As much as I'm locked out of!

There was the compensation, for example, of riding "back and forth all night on the ferry," as we have it in the utterly charming "Recuerdo."

As in *Renascence*, the volume closes with a group of sonnets, wholly in the mood of the book, but raising that mood to a more exquisite plane and to an immensely higher level of expression. The most perfect of the group of four is the first, perhaps the most deftly manipulated, sonnet she had written to this date.

Love, though for this you riddle me with darts,
And drag me at your chariot till I die,—
Oh, heavy prince! Oh, panderer of hearts!—
Yet hear me tell how in their throats they lie
Who shout you mighty: thick about my hair,
Day in, day out, your ominous arrows purr,
Who still am free, unto no querulous care
A fool, and in no temple worshiper!
I, that have bared me to your quiver's fire,
Lifted my face into its puny rain,
Do wreathe you Impotent to Evoke Desire
As you are Powerless to Elicit Pain!
(Now will the god, for blasphemy so brave,
Punish me, surely, with the shaft I crave!)

And one notes here not only the manipulation of the form, but also certain qualities which are to become increasingly characteristic of the author's sonnets: the classical allusions, the ellipsis of the pronouns, the inverted phrase order, the Shakespearean tonal echoes, and a certain weight of line rhythm that, allied to a profounder theme, gives in later sonnets a remarkable dignity and sonority.

A Few Figs From Thistles was not, after *Renascence*, a growth in poetic stature, but it gave its author a following, and it created what has become, unhappily or not, the Millay legend.

But the book remains one of the most important—perhaps the most important—of Miss Millay's volumes if we are to consider its contents as an indicator of what the poet's subsequent attitudes may be. Those attitudes were to find more dignified and more explicit treatment in later work, but their appearance for the first time here demands consideration, for they influenced not only much of the poet's more mature work, but the thought of a whole generation of readers as well. It is difficult, perhaps, to reconstruct now the impression these slight poems made on their public. Similar verse had been written before, but not by a woman. Here a woman was deliberately liberating herself from practically all conventional restrictions. She was being frivolous about sacred subjects, love and faithfulness and domesticity. She was saying that women could be quite as free as men, that they had in all human relationships as active a desire for expression as did men. She was saying to her astonished readers that women, as well as men, could sin and not be sorry, try as they would:

> . . . "One thing there's no getting by—
> I've been a wicked girl," said I;
> "But if I can't be sorry, why,
>   I might as well be glad!"

She was saying all this lightly, but she was none the less serious. The more startling expression of these ideas of

[19]

Edna St. Vincent Millay

freedom we find in later poems. *A Few Figs From Thistles* established for the author the right to speak—more important, the right for women to speak. She won with this book an audience to whom she was to address at a later date sterner lines. They were to read (and from the pen of a woman) the two sonnets in *The Harp-Weaver and Other Poems* beginning, "I, being born a woman and distressed" and "What lips my lips have kissed, and where and why"; they were to read as one of the most important works of their time *Fatal Interview*, a series of love sonnets whose theme was approached in a fashion once reserved for men. But by the time this latter volume appeared, the attitude of the public had changed. With *A Few Figs From Thistles* Miss Millay had converted an age; no woman writer is any longer faced with the necessity of restraint (save that demanded by art) in her treatment of any subject; no woman writer need withhold the truth in presenting her physical and intellectual approach to sex.

Though the tone of this volume of 1920 is uniformly light, the period between 1917 and 1921 was productive of other poems of a more serious nature. *Second April*, appearing in 1921, contains work published in periodicals as early as 1918, but the difference between the two volumes is striking. *Second April* represents, to some degree, a reaction. Gaiety and impudence are replaced by a delicate melancholy; the atmosphere of Greenwich Village bohemianism gives way to a nostalgia for the simplest countryside; the taunting daring of the earlier sonnets becomes here a romantic grief for the passing of love, the death of lovers. We have in this book another step in the advance to an attitude toward life that was slowly (but not willfully) crystallizing in Miss Millay's poetry. And we have here, too, for the first time definitely exhibited, the images and symbols which are to distinguish so much of the poet's subsequent work. These are drawn almost entirely from nature, images of the sea, and of stony upland meadows predominating. They are of the simplest sort. And though they are here less profoundly evocative than they become in *The Buck in the Snow*, in *Fatal Interview*, or in *Wine From These Grapes*, they are, however, capable of painting vividly the picture the author desires, and their use is always significant in relation to the poem in which they occur. They illustrate; they never confuse, either by being inaccurate symbols of the emotion to be conveyed, or by a multiplicity which (as was the case, ironically enough, with the Imagists) outweighs the thought and defeats its purpose by use of mutually destructive metaphor or simile. One of the greatest weaknesses of contemporary poetry is its misuse of imagery. By a great artist images, however brilliant, are closed in his poem like jewels in matrix, and (as some one has said of Plato's words) where they *are*, they *grew*. Too many of our present-day poets, striving to set down a thought not completely organized in their own minds, attempt to catch it in a net of images which bear no relation to one another save that they occur in the same poem. This weakness in the use of figures betrays on the one hand a lack of truly sensitive perception, and on the other a taste so "literary" and decorative as to be insignificant. It is this same taste that avoids simplicity, that is fearful of using a simile that (because the thing employed for the comparison is common) might seem to lack subtlety.

Miss Millay, even in *Second April*, was too good a poet to be lured into the use of elaborate and unmeaning figure. An early example of her restraint and its poignant effectiveness is to be found in "Elegy Before Death," in which

Edna St. Vincent Millay

a character, the "you" of the poem, is unmistakably, though obliquely, painted by the symbolical use of imagery. And in other poems from this volume, sorrel, eel-grass, shells, mullein, robins, rain-barrels, wild laurel, "sashes beset with snow," the "big surf," "weedy mussels," "her gowns," "her shoes"—one could extend the list—illustrate the simplicity of image, the extraordinary homeliness and unliterary quality which account in part for the wide appeal and much of the strength of Miss Millay's work.

Aspects of many poems in *Second April* provide interesting speculation: the curious mother-fantasies of "The Blue-Flag in the Bog," and "The Little Hill"; the beautiful tenderness and delicacy of emotion in the six poems in "Memorial to D. C.," the author's friend at Vassar; the increasingly frequent use of classical or traditional reference in symbols whose connotations have a renewed appeal in the poet's use of them (the Bean-stalk, Lesbia, Astolat and Elaine, the Muses, Persephone, Isolde, Helen) for they have all the freshness of a discovery; they are used as innocently, as un-self-consciously as the nature symbols already mentioned, and though we find in one poem

> Doubt no more that Oberon—
> Never doubt that Pan
> Lived, and played a reed, and ran
> After nymphs in a dark forest,

and in the next

> Keys and pennies
> Covered with tobacco;

> Anne, eat your breakfast;
> Dan, take your medicine;

yet they are all of perfect appropriateness, in such unaffected use recon-

Edna St. Vincent Millay

cilable, and the expression of a judicious choice. And then
to be considered is the ambitious "Ode to Silence," a poem
superbly musical, rivaling Tennyson (whom it faintly suggests) in its melody of vowel and consonant:

> In the black shade of what obsidian steep
> Stiffens the white narcissus numb with sleep

and in its use of repetition:

> There is a garden lying in a lull
> Between the mountains and the mountainous sea.

—but mostly
the poet cries for the sea or the stony field, being exiled
and "weary of words and people." There is a momentary
flare of the bright rockets of the previous volume in Sonnet ix,

> In me no lenten wicks watch out the night;
> I am the booth where Folly holds her fair;

but in Sonnet xii
the poet, "stern in my soul's chastity," renounces the

> puny fever and frail sweat
> of human love

for Pieria and the Singing Mountain.
The *Harp-Weaver and Other Poems,* published in 1923,
is in some respects the author's most uneven book. It contains poems that might well have been omitted, and
though it gives us one of her greatest sonnets, "Euclid
alone has looked on Beauty bare," one regrets the inclusion of such obvious and facilely sentimental pieces as
"Souvenir" with its

> Just a rainy day or two
> In a windy tower,
> That was all I had of you—

Edna St. Vincent Millay

These are balanced, however, with such fine lyrics as "Autumn Chant," "Feast," "Goose-Girl," and "Return from Town," though none of these surpasses the special beauty (in spite of the suspicion of smartness in the last stanza) of "Passer Mortuus Est" in *Second April*.

The title poem (which had previously been printed separately as a booklet, and on which the Pulitzer Prize Committee conferred its award) is a ballad of some length, directly, often movingly done, though in certain passages its pathos is somewhat perilously balanced on the brink of sentimentality. One feels that in comparison with the more real pathos of passages in the "Sonnets from an Ungrafted Tree," the "Harp-Weaver" tends to be specious. It is, however, an arresting example of contemporary ballad-writing, never attempting an imitation of the old ballads in language, irregular rhythm, or assonance, but creating from the plainest colloquialisms a presentation of mood and story analogous to that of the older ballads. The theme of mother love is rendered without too great an emphasis, and carries without difficulty the additional allegory of the child, who, ragged and cold, is clothed from the loom of the harp-strings, and warmed, at length, by an instrument of song.

There are other poems in the volume which display Miss Millay's talents to a greater degree. These are the lyrics recommended above, and such poems as "Never May the Fruit Be Plucked," "The Concert," the twenty-two unnamed sonnets, and the seventeen "Sonnets from an Ungrafted Tree," many of which represent a great advance in artistry and depth of emotion. The technique is here becoming more adjusted to the interpretation of fine differences in mood, the cadences are more subtle, the beat more refined. Much of Miss Millay's early work

Edna St. Vincent Millay

(particularly that composed in the simple, four-line stanza) has, so far as its musical quality is concerned, somewhat the monotony and looseness of texture of unison singing; in some of the poems under present consideration we come, so to speak, to a division of voices and to part singing. This change is notable in such poems as the Euclid sonnet (a study of which will reveal phrases that seem— so are their rhythms balanced—to speak and answer and join together again) or in "The Concert," with its short lines, staccato prose rhythms which accumulate one by one and then resolve themselves—by the magic of a run-over line or a long-withheld rhyme—into a sudden and melodious cadence:

> No, I will go alone.
> I will come back when it's over.
> Yes, of course I love you.
> No, it will not be long.
> Why may you not come with me?—
> You are too much my lover.
> You would put yourself
> Between me and song.

With the series of twenty-two unnamed sonnets begins the analysis of love which is continued in *Fatal Interview*. There is no parallel in American poetry for these two sequences, in the work of no other poet do we find so frankly set down, so honestly, so humanly, so nobly expressed the emotions of profane love. The sonnets range from grave to gay; they depict the pathos, the distress, the joy, the ennui, the pride, the blindness and the vision that characterize the changing moods of human relationship in love, ranging through all planes, from the sentiments of the bravest companionship to the stormiest desire. *Fatal Interview* will be considered later, but in these sonnets

Edna St. Vincent Millay

from *The Harp-Weaver* we have the opening movement
of a symphony of love music that, melancholy or
triumphant, is played out against a background where (we
are reminded) stretch ever,

> Black in the noon, the broad estates of Death.

But here it is the transience of love that is set down in
lines that sigh with resignation or "stir with quiet pain."
There is not that far-away thunder of pity and indignation
which we are to hear faintly in certain sonnets of *Fatal
Interview*, and more sharply in the author's superb sequence, "Epitaph for the Race of Man." In the present
group we have, rather, the pathos of a love that

> beholds, dismayed,
> The wind whereon its petals shall be laid.

But there is no self-pity here:

> Pity me not the waning of the moon,
> Nor that the ebbing tide goes out to sea,
> Nor that a man's desire is hushed so soon,
> And you no longer look with love on me. . . .
>
> Pity me that the heart is slow to learn
> What the swift mind beholds at every turn.

And with what
honesty, amounting almost to scorn and certainly to indifference—being so clearly understood and free from the
confusion of emotionalism—is Sonnet xviii set down:

> I, being born a woman and distressed
> By all the needs and notions of my kind,
> Am urged by your propinquity to find
> Your person fair, and feel a certain zest
> To bear your body's weight upon my breast:
> So subtly is the fume of life designed,

Edna St. Vincent Millay

To clarify the pulse and cloud the mind,
And leave me once again undone, possessed.
Think not for this, however, the poor treason
Of my stout blood against my staggering brain,
I shall remember you with love, or season
My scorn with pity,—let me make it plain:
I find this frenzy insufficient reason
For conversation when we meet again.

It is this superlative directness which distinguishes these poems as unique in the field of poetry written by women. What restraint, in the way of truth, Puritanism may have exercised on American literature at this time is here dealt a blow (and again in *Fatal Interview*) more telling than any propaganda on the subject might effect. It is a noteworthy fact, and one that Miss Millay has herself frequently pointed out, that at the present time most novels by front-rank writers that deal with *living*, with men and women—not as representatives of this or that race, or order, or group with theories to propound and prove, but men and women as *human beings* living together—these novels are coming from the pens of women. Propaganda, didacticism, social criticism, and ideas distort the picture of *life* as it is seen in the books of many men novelists of the day. This kind of truthfulness, that has no intention save *to tell the truth*, finds one of its earliest expressions in these sonnets by Miss Millay. In that sense the poems were revolutionary, but there is in them no suspicion of propaganda; they represent, in the sequence, merely one of the many aspects of love, and are given no more emphasis than is any other. The fact remains, however, that viewed from the outside, they mark a milestone in the conquest of prejudice and evasion. For this reason Sonnets xviii and xix in *The Harp-Weaver* have been given an amount of

Edna St. Vincent Millay

attention disproportionate to their place in the author's work, and their author has come to be regarded, in certain quarters, solely as the interpreter of a mood that occupies, relatively, a very small space in the canon of her work.

Included in this sequence, but scarcely related to it directly in subject-matter, is the now famous Euclid sonnet. This poem has been much praised as the finest sonnet written in America and one of the finest in the language. It is unique (in the author's work) in one striking aspect. Unlike many poets, Miss Millay has written nothing on the subject of poetry, has published no comment on the movements which have influenced verse in her time, has never (with one notable exception—a review of *Nets to Catch the Wind* by Elinor Wylie) reviewed a book of verse. The analysis of verse, the problems of technique, the credos of the schools, the questions of æsthetics have left her as spectator, never as participant. The futility of much of this type of writing becomes more and more evident to a poet who, like Miss Millay, is interested primarily in the simple and fundamental aspects of life, whose grasp of her material is such that her poetry reveals few, if any, mannerisms, no special vocabulary, no tricks of style. In the whole range of her poetry there is no poem which can justly be termed a *tour de force*. With how gusty a breath, then, is the web of dialectic swept away in the Euclid sonnet! No creative artist of any magnitude can long tolerate the prating of Beauty of the schools; he must

> seek release
> From dusty bondage into luminous air.

For Miss Millay Beauty hides not in the library nor in the lecture hall, not even, perhaps, in poetry; these places

[28]

Edna St. Vincent Millay

are too small, too confined; her massive sandal is set on deeper stone. And Beauty is free—even of love—as we see in a later sonnet from *Fatal Interview*:

> Beauty beyond all feathers that have flown
> Is free; you shall not hood her to your wrist,
> Nor sting her eyes, nor have her for your own
> In any fashion; beauty billed and kissed
> Is not your turtle; tread her like a dove—
> She loves you not; she never heard of love.

The "Sonnets from an Ungrafted Tree" present a new aspect of Miss Millay's talent, but they have been overshadowed by the more highly colored and provocative series already discussed. This present group of seventeen false sonnets (the last line of each is lengthened to seven feet) has received insufficient attention. They paint a *genre* picture, a New England scene for which it would be difficult to find a parallel. The story of the wife who, loving him not at all, returns to her husband as he lies dying, who cleans the neglected house, who sits alone, proud, avoiding even the grocer's boy, awaiting the death of this man who

> had come into her life when anybody
> Would have been welcome, so in need was she,

is set down with an accuracy, a colorless and toneless quality, that convey painfully the woman's numb, inarticulate conflict, her relentless sense of duty and her fright. The whole is sharpened by skillfully chosen detail:

> The winter rain
> Splashed in the painted butter-tub outside,

. . . .

Edna St. Vincent Millay

(That day when dust is on the wood-box floor,
And some old catalogue, and a brown, shrivelled apple core.)

.   .   .   .

the grinding of a backing wagon wheel

.   .   .   .

To gather in, before the line gave way,
Garments, board-stiff, that galloped on the blast

.   .   .   .

She had kept that kettle boiling all night long, for company.

.   .   .   .

The axe was nodding in the block. . . .

But, beyond the story,
beyond the vividness of the atmosphere, lies a poignant
sympathy with the woman, who, loving beauty, loving love,
has been frustrated in both. There is little bitterness in
the telling, there is little pity even, but one is conscious
of a hard knot of suppressed anger that weighs heavily
on the heart. Not until *The Buck In The Snow* is that
anger released, in a volume that might well have placed
upon its title page the lines found in the middle of the
book,

Cruel of heart, lay down my song.

.   .   .   .

Not for you was the pen bitten,
And the mind wrung, and the song written.

[30]

Edna St. Vincent Millay

With the exception of *Wine From These Grapes*, *The Buck In The Snow*, 1928, is, in range of subject-matter and treatment, the author's finest book. Five years elapsed between its publication and that of its predecessor, *The Harp-Weaver*, but between these two dates the author had written *The King's Henchman* (which will be considered elsewhere in this essay) and had joined her name and her talent to the cause of Sacco and Vanzetti at the time of their trial. At least five of the poems in *The Buck in the Snow*—"Song," "Winter Night," "Counting Out Rhyme," "West Country Song," and "When Cæsar Fell," show the influence of the matter and manner of *The King's Henchman* and two, at least, "Justice Denied in Massachusetts," and "Hangman's Oak," are the direct comment of a noble spirit writing, in anger and in anguish, of that injustice which many have felt characterized the trial of the two ' Italians.

But there are other poems than these (which might be called, in the highest sense of the term, occasional) to lend distinction to the volume. The whole book sounds with a deeper tone; there is through it less of the ringing of bells and the voluptuous or plaintive crying of violins. The lines vibrate with the rich, profound, slow movement of 'cellos and, at times, the roll of drums. The emotion has grown wise; the quick thought, one feels, has become meditation. Not that flashes of the gay indomitable fighting spirit of the earlier volumes are missing. "Moriturus" shouts with a love, a greed, for life; with an almost desperate haste is death named away, called little, called nothing, though the poem ends with a struggle that suggests Death as a formidable antagonist:

> I shall put up a fight,
> I shall take it hard.

Edna St. Vincent Millay

With his hand on my mouth
He shall drag me forth,
Shrieking to the south
And clutching at the north.

Anything, cries the poet, rather

Than go with Death
Where nothing good,

Not even the thrust
Of the summer gnat,
Consoles the dust
For being that.

The poem is in many points typical of Miss Millay's attitude. She has written no poems on death; one finds nowhere in her work that anatomy of dying to be found in the pages of many contemporary poets; her poems are concerned with living; and life deserted, rather than Death embraced, forms her theme. The zest for living set down so forcefully in "Moriturus" pervades every poem Miss Millay has written. It is shown in many ways. A strong pulse beats through each line; no poem is thinned, no line is cooled to the temperature of icy and passionless comment. Every phrase, every image is bold with love for what is living; nothing is invented; there is no furnishing forth of intellectualistic design; images are drawn from sources warmed by human contact, seen by the eyes and felt by the hands—the rooms have been lived in, so to speak, and anything less than the human touch fails to satisfy this poet. It is all a part of her passion for truth, for absolute sincerity of statement unadorned and unliterary, lacking the deceit of false melody, or the mystery attained at the expense of meaning, logical or poetical, by obscure expression or recondite allusion. Truth, said

[32]

Edna St. Vincent Millay

a great man, also has its roof and bed and board. Miss Millay has never sought truth where there was not also life. Such a quest as hers needs strength—strength to admit joy, grief, fatigue, disillusionment. Such strength will not pour oil on troubled waters, will not avoid sharp corners, will not deceive, will not compromise—will resort to none of the evasions and soft escapes of the man who would keep life smooth and unruffled because he is afraid of conflict.

Miss Millay has written poems that record a boundless joy; she has written poems that are full of despair. She is too honest to clothe Death in the flowing draperies of some twilight mystery; too intelligent to accept the speciousness of the professional optimist, be he cleric or scientist. Thomas Hardy greatly admired the poetry of Edna St. Vincent Millay. This is readily comprehensible when one realizes (in the words of I. A. Richards) that Hardy is "the poet who has most steadily refused to be comforted. The comfort of forgetfulness, the comfort of beliefs, he has put both of these away. Hence his singular preoccupation with death. . . ." Hardy never expressed the thought better than did Miss Millay in "Dirge Without Music."

I am not resigned to the shutting away of loving hearts in the
　　　　hard ground.
So it is, and so it will be, for so it has been, time out of mind:
Into the darkness they go, the wise and the lovely. Crowned
With lilies and with laurel they go; but I am not resigned.

Nor did he ever state with a more effective irony the death of the gods than did Miss Millay in her sonnet "To Jesus on His Birthday":

The stone the angel rolled away with tears
Is back upon your mouth these thousand years.

Edna St. Vincent Millay

—or attack cowardice with a sharper cry than in the "Sonnet to Gath":

> Dust in an urn long since, dispersed and dead
> Is great Apollo; and the happier he;
> Since who amongst you all would lift a head
> At a god's radiance on the mean door-tree,
> Saving to run and hide your dates and bread,
> And cluck your children in about your knee?

But her lips are braver than his—wiser perhaps—when she speaks in another sonnet:

> This is my testament: that we are taken;
> Our colours are as clouds before the wind;
> Yet for a moment stood the foe forsaken,
> Eying Love's favour to our helmet pinned;
> Death is our master,—but his seat is shaken;
> He rides victorious,—but his ranks are thinned, . . .

And what is all this except an immense courage, a love of life so overwhelming that she can write

> Life, were thy pains as are the pains of hell,
> So hardly to be borne, yet to be borne,
> And all thy boughs more grim with wasp and thorn
> Then armoured bough stood ever; too chill to spell
> With the warm tongue, and sharp with broken shell
> Thy ways, whereby in wincing haste forlorn
> The desperate foot must travel, blind and torn,
> Yet must I cry,—So be it; it is well.

The poems on the Sacco-Vanzetti case ("Justice Denied in Massachusetts," and "Hangman's Oak") included here, the memorial sonnets printed in 1930 in the *New Republic*, and included in *Wine From These Grapes*, the article called "Fear" in the *Outlook* in 1927 are the record of a poet's hatred of injustice. These poems and the letter sent to the Governor of Massachusetts the hour before

[34]

Edna St. Vincent Millay

the execution of these men occupy a place in that history of our time which concerns itself with truth. How dreadful is the calm of these poems; how deadly the implications:

Sour to the fruitful seed
Is the cold earth under this cloud,
Fostering quack and weed, we have marched upon but cannot
      conquer;
We have bent the blades of our hoes against the stalks of them.

.   .   .   .

The sun . . .
We shall not feel it again.
We shall die in darkness, and be buried in the rain.

.   .   .   .

Brother, I said to the air beneath the bough
    Whence he had swung,
It will not be long for any of us now;
    We do not grow young.

It will not be long for the knotter of ropes, not long
    For the sheriff or for me,
Or for any of them that came five hundred strong
    To see you swing from a tree.

Side by side together in the belly of Death
    We sit without hope,
You, and I, and the mother that gave you breath,
    And the tree, and the rope.

And the letter, composed in an anguish of haste that only an artist could feel who essayed in an hour's time that perfection of expression which would move with its truth and its beauty a stubborn and a frightened man,

[35]

Edna St. Vincent Millay

may well be given here as further proof of the passion which moved the author to participate in the demonstration which marked the period of the trial.

Arthur Garfield Hays gives an account of those painful hours:[1]

"Miss Millay had conferred with the Governor during the day. She had not sought to argue the evidence. She had related to the Governor a story she had heard as a child, of the reason for the abolition of capital punishment in the state of Maine.

"Edna St. Vincent Millay retired to the next room to write a letter and at twenty minutes to twelve brought in the following:

"YOUR EXCELLENCY,

During my interview with you this afternoon, I called to your attention a distressing instance of the miscarriage of justice in a neighboring state. I suggested that, for all of your careful weighing of the evidence, for all your courage in the face of threats and violent words, for all your honest conviction that these men are guilty, you, no less than the Governor of Maine in my story, who was so tragically mistaken, are but human flesh and spirit, and that it is human to err.

Tonight, with the world in doubt, with this commonwealth drawing into its lungs with every breath the difficult air of doubt, with the eyes of Europe turned westward upon Massachusetts and upon the whole United States in distress and harrowing doubt —are you still so sure? For, indeed, your spirit, however strong, is but the frail spirit of man. Have you no need, in this hour, of a spirit greater than your own?

Think back. Think back a long time. Which way

[1] See appendix B.

would He have turned, this Jesus of your faith? Oh, not the way in which your feet are set!

You promised me, and I believed you truly, that you would think of what I said. I exact of you this promise now. Be for a moment alone with yourself. look inward upon yourself for a moment. Which way would He have turned, this Jesus of your faith?

I cry to you with a million voices; answer our doubt! Exert the clemency which your high office affords!

There is need in Massachusetts of a great man to-night. It is not yet too late for you to be that man.

EDNA ST. VINCENT MILLAY."[1]

The Buck In The Snow contains other poems than those concerned with the author's reaction to injustice. In contrast, and rendered more touching, perhaps, by that contrast, are such lovely poems as "Song," with its murmuring, indefinable, and withdrawn melancholy:

> Gone, gone again is Summer the lovely,
>   Gone again on every side,
> Lost again like a shining fish from the hand
>   Into the shadowy tide.

There has entered into this volume in certain poems a note as of muted strings that is very beautiful. We find it in "West Country Song." We have it again in "Cameo," which in its clarity suggests the "Ode on a Grecian Urn," and in the "Hardy Garden" where only the enduring, the perennial flowers shall be planted as maidens to unending love. This subdued hum pervades "Dawn" and "Northern April." Perhaps the most notably beautiful of all the poems in this volume is the title poem itself, that picture

[1] *Let Freedom Ring*, Arthur Garfield Hays. New York, Boni and Liveright, 1928. Pp. 337-338.

that has so much the quality, the soft, the subdued, but fluid movement of a Japanese print; but one senses here the tang of New England air and the smell of hemlock, and the emotion is Miss Millay's, the theme hers:

Life, looking out attentive from the eyes of the doe.

The volume concludes with seven sonnets that form a surprisingly complete epitome, set down in her favorite form, of the author's themes and her matured point of view, and one suspects they were thus gathered in one place to be, in miniature, the record of her attitudes.

The year 1928 saw, also, in the Anniversary number of the St. Louis *Post-Dispatch*, the publication of the sonnet sequence "Epitaph for the Race of Man." These ten sonnets, with eight others, are included in the author's most recent volume, and will be discussed later. It is, however, worthy of note at this point that these sonnets—so striking in their departure from Miss Millay's usual theme—antedate the *Fatal Interview* series, and provide an answer (if one be needed) to the criticism in some quarters that Miss Millay was, poetically, standing still, that she had only one very personal thing to say, and that, magnificent as *Fatal Interview* might be, it was merely a repetition of what she had said many times before, and only proved again how tightly she was chained to her own individual emotions.

This first printing of "Epitaph for the Race of Man" was followed three years later, in 1931, by a volume of sonnets, *Fatal Interview*. This book has been the subject of as much critical acclaim and of more popular appreciation than any other volume of major poetry in our time. Here we shall consider it in certain aspects only, after

Edna St. Vincent Millay

pointing out in passing that it represents Miss Millay's highest expression of her favorite theme of love. The sequence contains lines which epitomize practically every phase of the whole range of her work.

> Youth, have no pity; leave no farthing here
> For age to invest in compromise and fear,

which was the theme of *A Few Figs From Thistles*. And once more her gauntlet is flung down in defiance of Time in

> Never shall he inherit what was mine.
> When Time and all his tricks have done their worst,
> Still will I hold you dear, and him accurst.

Her own special quality she defines here:

> . . . being like my mother the brown earth
> Fervent, and full of gifts, and free from guile,

Her descriptive powers have never surpassed in vividness, the scene, so typical of her New England:

> on a salty day
> When inland woods were pushed by winds that flung them
> Hissing to leeward like a ton of spray,
> I thought how off Matinicus the tide
> Came pounding in, came running through the Gut,
> While from the Rock the warning whistle cried,
> And children whimpered, and the doors blew shut;
> There in the autumn when the men go forth,
> With slapping skirts the island women stand
> In gardens stripped and scattered, peering north,
> With dahlia tubers dripping from the hand:

That independence of spirit in love is proclaimed in

> What you cannot do
> Is bow me down, that have been loved by you.

Edna St. Vincent Millay

But a triumphant pride, sung in many poems, lies in the superb image,

> bearing as I bear
> Love like a burning city in the breast.

All the lyric gift which had composed the singing lines of scores of poems is supremely evident in that wonderful last sonnet which begins:

> Oh, sleep forever in the Latmian cave,
> Mortal Endymion, darling of the Moon!

and ends with the final comment on that profane love which has found in this sequence what well may prove to be its ultimate expression:

> she wanders mad, being all unfit
> For mortal love, that might not die of it.

The power of these sonnets is enhanced by their dramatic arrangement. The sequence has the narrative quality of a superb monologue, rising to a series of climaxes, withdrawing for reflection and readjustment. The shiftings of mood have a reality of sequence that cannot be disputed: the joy and triumph of the beginning, the foreboding of Sonnet xxxiv; the anguish of the last line of xxxviii; the bitterness of the blow acknowledged in xxxix; the magnificent common sense of xlvi; the persuasive rationalization of xlvii and xlviii; the proud yet wistful melancholy of li, and the last sonnet of all, in which the alchemy of time has transmuted the whole experience into a radiant and satisfying definition.

After *Fatal Interview* Miss Millay's masterly control of the sonnet form awaited only a subject of sufficient magnitude to reach its culmination. That subject had already been discovered and treated in the ten sonnets (unfor-

[40]

Edna St. Vincent Millay

tunately at that time little known) of "Epitaph for the Race of Man." The series was now completed and we have the magnificent panorama of Man's tragic history which is included in *Wine From These Grapes*, 1934.

In these eighteen sonnets we have the noblest theme to which Miss Millay has devoted her talent. She has turned from the individual to the race, and with a sense of proportion attained only through the far-sighted vision of history and science, has not only summarized in eighteen chapters the biological, the eventual, the emotional record of

> Man, with his singular laughter, his droll tears,

but has framed this in a form and with a power that illustrate the extraordinary illumination art can give (and in how brief a space!) to the meaning of the vast materials which such a theme must survey. Under a title which has its own grandeur we have, then, her profound vision of that race which grew and warred and died, at length, by its own hand. The sequence opens with a picture of the earth deserted.

> Before this cooling planet shall be cold,
> Long, long before the music of the Lyre,
> Like the faint roar of distant breakers rolled
> On reefs unseen, when wind and flood conspire
> To drive the ship inshore—long, long, I say,
> Before this ominous humming hits the ear,
> Earth will have come upon a stiller day,
> Man and his engines be no longer here.
> High on his naked rock the mountain sheep
> Will stand alone against the final sky,
> Drinking a wind of danger new and deep,
> Staring on Vega with a piercing eye,
> And gather up his slender hooves and leap
> From crag to crag down Chaos, and so go by.

Edna St. Vincent Millay

Follows with stark and unappealable indictments the history of the race:

> Peace at the void's heart through the wordless night,
> A lamb cropping the awful grasses, grazed;
> Earthward the trouble lies, where strikes his light
> At dawn industrious Man, and unamazed
> Goes forth to plough, flinging a ribald stone
> At all endeavour alien to his own.

The blame is placed; not in heaven lies the seed of this terror—"Earthward the trouble lies" with Man

> "flinging a ribald stone
> At all endeavour alien to his own."

There is an unconquerable strength in this man who combats and survives whatever disaster of storm and flood Earth may fling upon him. For a moment man was a friend of man; from mutual disaster sprang a reluctant, a timorous and distrustful, brotherhood. But Man, so strong to withstand the "headless Force" of Natural Law, was weak before "the unkindness in his brother's eyes," and what portents of eventual annihilation the inquiring mind might discover in "whistling space" could be matched in immediate "intimate conflict" with his neighbor. In the concluding sonnet, with what dreadful pity is the last line written, the pity of knowledge, the pity of one who had seen a world at war, even more sadly a world at peace, and therein had seen a vision of the end.

Here lies, and none to mourn him but the sea,
That falls incessant on the empty shore,
Most various Man, cut down to spring no more;
Before his prime, even in his infancy
Cut down, and all the clamour that was he,
Silenced; and all the riveted pride he wore,
A rusted iron column whose tall core

Edna St. Vincent Millay

The rains have tunnelled like an aspen tree.
Man, doughty Man, what power has brought you low,
That heaven itself in arms could not persuade
To lay aside the lever and the spade
And be as dust among the dusts that blow?
Whence, whence the broadside? whose the heavy blade? . . .
Strive not to speak, poor scattered mouth; I know.

These two great sonnet sequences, *Fatal Interview* and
"Epitaph for the Race of Man," are the crowning achievement of Miss Millay's work to the present time, and together they provide one of the brightest glories of
American poetry. They afford contrasts of great interest:
the sonnets of *Fatal Interview* are in the Shakespearean
form; those of "Epitaph for the Race of Man" (save two
whose octaves are Elizabethan) in the Petrarchian. The
author is equally the master of each. The effortless perfection of form, the opulence of language, the felicity and
variety of the music, the poise of the accent, the crescendo
and diminuendo within each sonnet, the unmistakable
legato which marks the control of the great artist—all these
are, even upon a first reading, strikingly evident in each
sequence. The strongly contrasting themes, the one in-
tensely lyric and personal, the other epic in its range, narrative, impersonal (but into which pity and pride must
creep) offer opportunities for a richness of significant
image that have been fully accepted and fulfilled. The
images in *Fatal Interview* are bounded by the intimacy of
the emotion:

> Your look that is today my east and west.

And though the gods are called from heaven, it is to wit-
ness "the red heart crumpled in the side." In "Epitaph
for the Race of Man," the images are of space and magnitude; they stride "like the sun into the middle sky."

[43]

Edna St. Vincent Millay

Images of the watcher whose vision is measured only by the limits of recorded time, they are completely detached and impersonal. One is scarcely conscious that this is human vision; rather it seems the inevitable ticking of history, in flashes of profound brilliance and clarity. Miss Millay has, in *Fatal Interview*, mingled with consummate skill figures and symbols drawn from the most various sources—classical, mediæval, contemporary; land, sea, and air, and their four seasons—and uses each with such astonishing ease and freshness that the reader is persuaded he is encountering even the oldest of them for the first time. As purely creative as the most striking novelty of invention is this making of new beauty and symbolism out of old. "The slopes of Venus and her boy" glimmer before one's eyes; "The brooch of Troilus pinned upon the Greek" is as moving a picture as the vivid

> How drowned in love and weedily washed ashore,

In "Epitaph for the Race of Man" the imagery is of heaven and earth; the stars and the tumultuous teeming land provide figures of a magnitude commensurate with the theme of the sequence, yet by no one of them, brilliant as they are, is the reader moved to a disproportionate attention; their vividness as picture is subordinated to their value as *poetry*, and they become, by the miraculous transubstantiation of great art, the very poem itself. It is in this respect (among others) that one may compare Miss Millay's art in the sonnet to Shakespeare's: for, like his, her expression is metaphorical to the highest degree and her symbols have become, in themselves, poems.

But *Wine From These Grapes* contains other beauties than those of "Epitaph for the Race of Man." This book has stemmed from *The Buck in the Snow*. The austerities

[44]

Edna St. Vincent Millay

of form and expression in that volume are here fulfilled; the personal emotion is less accented—there are no love poems in the book—than in any previous volume of the author's. There is a most marked change too, in the writing, notably in the rhymed forms, where a striking "tightening up" of the line attains to a kind of tautness which drives the meaning home as sharply as an arrow is shot from a stretched bow string. And there is a new note, not readily definable, in the more descriptive pieces. The New England scenes, the hills, the stony pastures, the weeds and trees which in so many of Miss Millay's poems have been brought to life, with a startling distinctness, as background, as illustration, as contrast, carved out with a kind of woody (but not wooden) strength, as by a hand that knew well its tools and the feel of its material—these are, in her latest poems, made, somehow, and for the first time, *dear*. The author seems herself to have sensed this new quality of feeling in "From a Train Window":

Precious in the January morning the shabby fur of the cat-
tails by the stream.
The farmer driving his horse to the feed-store for a sack of
cracked corn
Is not in haste; there is no whip in the socket.

How dramatically these scenes may be used is proved in "In the Grave No Flower"; how moving they may be is to be seen in "Spring in the Garden," a poem in its rhythm, imagery, and sharpness of emotion very typical of its author:

And I fear that not a root in all this heaving sea
Of land, has nudged you where you lie, has found
Patience and time to direct you, numb and stupid as you still
must be
From your first winter under ground.

[45]

Edna St. Vincent Millay

Many of the lyrics are in mood and thought associated with aspects of "Epitaph for the Race of Man." They deal bitterly or resignedly with the stupidities, gently or with a fine melancholy with the weaknesses of that race whose course has been traced so shrewdly in the sonnets. "Apostrophe to Man," with its stinging whip-lash ending,

Breed, crowd, encroach, expand, expunge yourself, die out,
Homo called *sapiens*.

illustrates the former; "On the Wide Heath," and "My Spirit, Sore from Marching," the latter. But for all the author's clear vision of the littleness of man, her zest for life rests undiminished. That theme which impregnates Miss Millay's least line sings with a new sturdiness in "Conscientious Objector":

I shall die, but that is all that I shall do for Death.

.   .   .   .

I will not tell him the whereabouts of my friends nor of my
    enemies either.
Though he promise me much, I will not map him the route
    to any man's door.

—and in "Lines for a Gravestone," the theme is restated, this time from the lips of the dead:

> Here lieth one who would resign
> Gladly his lot, to shoulder thine.
> Give me thy coat; get into mine.

But Miss Millay is well aware that mere living is not, alone, a sufficient recompense for the futility, greed, and broken pledges that so characterize our existence; and her answer is ready:

[46]

Edna St. Vincent Millay

Draw from the shapeless moment
Such pattern as you can;
And cleave henceforth to Beauty;
Expect no more from man.

This book gives, in many ways, the finishing touches to the canvas Miss Millay has, through her previous volumes, been painting. One feels that in these poems are to be found those colors which were perhaps lacking before, those which aid the perspective: the result is an adjustment of planes, a new proportion, a bringing into focus of details that combine to form a mass integral and complete. We know now the range and the predominating tones of the artist's palette:

Stained with these grapes I shall lie down to die.

II

The poetic plays of Miss Millay contain far less of the fundamental drama which we follow with such interest and sympathy in *Fatal Interview*, or even in the "Sonnets from an Ungrafted Tree." Of the author's five plays, two are of importance: *Aria da Capo*, and *The King's Henchman*. Of the others, *The Princess Marries the Page* is pervaded with that charm and gaiety—very feminine in its quality of archness—that Miss Millay has reserved for her lighter work in dramatic form. The verse is frequently delicious in its freshness, the scene and action delightful in their delicacy. The value of *Two Slatterns and a King* lies largely in its clever adaptation of the manner of the mediæval interlude. *The Lamp and the Bell*, a five-act tragedy in blank verse, is more ambitious in plan and execution, and more successful. Here the verse has a greater richness; the rhythms approach more nearly the move-

[47]

ment of speech, though the reader is conscious of padding. The constantly changing scenes and their brevity serve also to weaken the desired note of tragedy. In fact, it is only when we come to *Aria da Capo* and *The King's Henchman* that Miss Millay's work in dramatic form can be considered seriously. *Aria da Capo* is a triumph. With the lightest imaginable touch, with the gayest chatter, with scarcely any emphasis at all, this "tragedy with comic properties" is a devastating indictment of man's folly, his greed, his quarrels, his war-like games. Its irony is exquisitely done: vain and frivolous Columbine, gay and cynical Pierrot, poor simple Corydon and Thyrsis play and know not what they play. The silly shepherds are in a moment overwhelmed with their own game. The lines fly like brightly colored arrows; they cut, like little sabers, to the heart. The movement is wholly swift, and neatly molded—a lovely filigree through which glitters a bejeweled sermon. More than once has Miss Millay been characterized as a "preacher." The comment is only partly true. In "Sonnet to Gath," in "To Jesus on His Birthday," in "Justice Denied in Massachusetts," and in "Hangman's Oak" we have an outraged anger that, like a Puritan divine, lashes a frightened and silent audience. In *Aria da Capo* we have a sermon in tinsel, a whipping in gauze and confetti. So brightly does this poet preach, so winning the voice and the word, that the lesson remains.

The King's Henchman represents the final of several ideas for the libretto, to a score by Deems Taylor, of an opera commissioned by the Metropolitan Opera Company. As a libretto it may well be unique; as a poetic play it contains elements of great interest. The scene—tenth-century England—provides a colorful setting for a drama of simple and undelayed movement admirably adapted to

Edna St. Vincent Millay

opera, where plot of any considerable complexity would prove unwieldy. The text contains passages of high lyric beauty (the love poetry of Act Two, for example), musical in phrase and line, and with varying rhythm equally pleasant to the reader or the singer. The play has been widely read as a play, and, divorced from its score, still retains its integrity as a dramatic work. The illusion is heightened not a little by the author's fidelity to Anglo-Saxon speech and rhythms.[1] The difficulty of the task is obvious; and the honesty of the scholarship, the sensitiveness to the spirit of the period—particularly in its more colloquial aspects, which are always lively—exhibit a fortunate alliance of research and creative imagination. One of the finest passages in the play, illustrating as it does the dramatic quality of the verse and its adaptability to musical expression, is the Lament for the Untimely Dead. The lines can be extracted from their setting and read as a complete poem without the context:

EADGAR

The axe ringeth in the wood.

LORDS

And thou liest here.

EADGAR

The boat shoves off from shore. The child of the boatman dippeth her hand in the sunny water of the sea.

LORDS

And thou liest here.

---

[1] In the endeavor to create an atmosphere suggesting tenth-century England, and especially to make the speech sound as much as possible as it sounded then, Miss Millay used in *The King's Henchman* no word some form of which was not in use in England before the Norman Conquest.

Edna St. Vincent Millay

EADGAR

The horse standeth in the smithy door with lifted hoof, and
  shivers against the flies.

LORDS

And thou liest here.

CHORUS OF ALL THE PEOPLE

Woe-lo-woe!
Was it the wind in the tree?
He that spoke but now is no longer in the room.
Forth-farèd is he.

Miss Millay has not yet done her finest work in the field
of poetic drama, and it is to be hoped that she will again
turn her attention to composition in this form. She has,
indubitably, the power of dramatic and concentrated expression (not only her plays, but nearly every poem of
hers proves this), a sense of rapid but controlled movement, and a delicate appreciation of mood. *The King's
Henchman* offers, also, ample evidence that she can draw
a character. Her chief weakness lies in a failure to provide
and elucidate the strong motivations, based on character,
that would, by their mutual conflicts, create a dramatic
situation, but this weakness is probably to be excused on
the score of the exigencies of the commissions which the
plays fulfilled.

III

One of the most impressive characteristics of Miss Millay's poetry is its honesty. One can quite literally believe
what she says. Her entire literary expression points to this

conclusion; in no poem is the reader conscious of a pose, in no poem does art—or artfulness—stand in the way of truth. But it takes time to learn to be honest, a long time to discover truth, and one may scarcely expect to find a poet, save in his mature work, escaping contradictions, hesitation, and generalities. Miss Millay is, to an unusual degree, free from these weaknesses. One could list with little difficulty her attitudes toward life, so deliberately, so succinctly has she set them down. A few examples will illustrate the point:

Life, were thy pains as are the pains of hell,
Yet must I cry,—So be it; it is well.

. . . .

Earth's fiery core alone can feed the bough
That blooms between Orion and the Plough.

. . . .

Take up the song; forget the epitaph.[1]

. . . .

There is something to be learned, I guess, from looking at the
dead leaves under the living tree;

. . . .

Something to be learned—though I was ever a ten-o'clock
scholar at this school—
Even perhaps by me.

[1] It may be noted here that the sonnet of which this is the last line, "The Pioneer," was written in memory of Inez Milholland, the feminist leader. The note printed with the poem in *The Buck in the Snow* makes no mention of this fact, but is otherwise accurate.

Edna St. Vincent Millay

But my heart goes out to the oak-leaves that are the last to
    sigh
"Enough," and loose their hold;

.   .   .   .

Expect no more from man.

.   .   .   .

Strive not to speak, poor scattered mouth; I know.

What have we here? Acceptance, courage, hope, disillusionment, and great pity—a list developing in a quite understandable sequence— the last, the great pity, more to be noted in *Wine From These Grapes* than in any previous volume. It permeates "The Fledgling," "In the Grave No Flower," "Spring in the Garden," "On the Wide Heath," and forms the noble conclusion of "Epitaph for the Race of Man."

Much might be written on what lies behind these attitudes, these strong likes and dislikes, unqualified and often harsh. In Miss Millay's poems life is no mystery; nature is here about us, most movingly described and most intimately related to our moods, but it is never analyzed, never questioned. No attempt is made to explain, to search out the key to life or to the universe. After *Renascence*, the poems contain little wonder and no surprise. Seldom is anything stated as a problem. What problem there may have been was solved before the poem was written, and we have the conclusion clearly, often sharply, stated; the steps in the solution, the doubts as to the answer, are not even suggested, much less made (as so often with some poets) into poems. She waits until she can give the definite attitude, without vagueness, without hesitancy (we are

Edna St. Vincent Millay

speaking, of course, only of those poems in which an expression of attitude is required). We have, for example, no treatment, however tentative, of the theme of human history until "Epitaph for the Race of Man," but when it does appear we have it all complete, and there is no possible doubt as to the author's attitude. This refusal to commit oneself until an opinion has been formed, or a necessity arises, can be traced to New England—even specifically to Maine.

Far from being hasty, dogmatic statement, far from being didactic, or insistent, or repetitious, these attitudes, with their common sense, their expression in the traditional forms of verse, their earthy inborn wisdom allied to a strength based on the steady accretions of comprehended experience, may in their turn be traced (without undue resort to such distinctions) to the conservatism of woman. It is the actuality of this "comprehended experience" (the reader is aware of it more, perhaps, through feeling than through analysis) that gives to Miss Millay's verse a nearness, an intimacy, a reality not common in contemporary verse. Nothing has been chilled in passing through the mold of art. Life has lost none of its warmth, none of its color, and, in spite of the perfection of expression, none, indeed, of its ruggedness. Nothing stands between the reader and the poem. The impact of the poetry is direct and instantaneous. This directness is masculine. Only in the early work is there an insinuating appeal. The feminine quality that exists in the later work shows largely in the hatred of cruelty, in an occasional poem on childhood, in a kind of philosophical *waiting*, in, at times, a superior and punishing anger (as in "Apostrophe to Man"), when mankind is behaving like a stupid, conceited, and destructive child.

[53]

Edna St. Vincent Millay

There is a school of criticism that would search behind these attitudes, these persistent themes, behind the fearlesssly chosen subject and its fearless expression, for the personal experience and the character of the author. Such a quest has little to do with poetry (which can be judged only on its own merits whatever may be its source) and this essay will not fall into that error, at least—an error which has taken poetry out of the field of art and moved it (even for the purpose of literary criticism) into the case-books of the psychologists. What can be said here, and what is infinitely more important, is, first, that in Miss Millay's poetry the American scenes she knows are set down with a truth unsurpassed in American poetry. No poet has made his reader feel more poignantly the sea and the upland meadows. Nowhere are the common grasses so close to the hand and foot. These scenes are written in deep love, and at times with an almost Virgilian lyricism.

Second, that no writer of our time has so completely mastered the form that has taxed the powers of the greatest poets in the language as Miss Millay in her two great sonnet sequences—not only the form, but the matter as well; for though *Fatal Interview* as a series of love sonnets has scarcely a peer save that of Shakespeare's, "Epitaph for the Race of Man" stands unparalleled in the scope and grandeur of its theme.

Third, that American literature owes to Miss Millay what amounts to a whole new field of expression for its women writers, the field of unrestricted, unprejudiced discussion of personal relationships, giving to women a position in literature on a par with that of any man.

And fourth, that, great as her accomplishment has been, one senses more to come; the power increases, not only

Edna St. Vincent Millay

along lines already determined, but in new directions as well, Criticism, weighing the variety of theme, the plane of the emotion and its truth, the nobility of expression in Miss Millay's finest work, must find that work unmatched by that of any woman poet in the history of any literature.

APPENDICES

APPENDIX A

THE following early poems of Miss Millay, taken from the pages of *St. Nicholas*, show with what control she was, even at this early age, writing verse. Already the dramatic situation appeals to her: already an individual style and vocabulary are discernible. But even here there seems to be little evidence of any striking influence. Perhaps (knowing from her farewell letter to the St. Nicholas League how much she admired Browning) we can detect traces of his Monologues, but the connection is superficial, of general form only.

H. L. C.

THE LAND OF ROMANCE

(Age 14, Gold Badge, St. Nicholas League)

"Show me the road to Romance!" I cried, and he raised his head;
"I know not the road to Romance, child. 'Tis a warm, bright way,"
    he said,
"And I trod it once with one whom I loved,—with one who is long
    since dead.
But now—I forget,—Ah! The way would be long without that other
    one,"
And he lifted a thin and trembling hand, to shield his eyes from
    the sun.

"Show me the road to Romance!" I cried, but she did not stir,
And I heard no sound in the low-ceil'd room save the spinning-
    wheel's busy whirr.
Then came a voice from the down-bent head, from the lips that I
    could not see,
"Oh! Why do you seek for Romance? And why do you trouble me?
Little care I for your fancies. They will bring you no good," she said,
"Take the wheel that stands in the corner, and get you to work
    instead."

[59]

Edna St. Vincent Millay

Then came one with steps so light that I had not heard their tread,
"I know where the road to Romance is. I will show it you," she said.
She slipped her tiny hand in mine, and smiled up into my face,
And lo! A ray of the setting sun shone full upon the place,
The little brook danced adown the hill and the grass sprang up
    anew,
And tiny flowers peeped forth as fresh as if newly washed with dew.

A little breeze came frolicking by, cooling the heated air,
And the road to Romance stretched on before, beckoning, bright
    and fair.
And I knew that just beyond it, in the hush of the dying day,
The mossy walls and ivied towers of the land of Romance lay.
The breath of dying lilies haunted the twilight air,
And the sob of a dreaming violin filled the silence everywhere.

E. Vincent Millay

Conclusion of unpublished poem, age about 15

Let me not shout into the world's great ear
Ere I have something for the world to hear.
Then let my message like an arrow dart
And pierce a way into the world's great heart.

FRIENDS

(Age 17, Cash Prize, St. Nicholas League)

I

(He)

I've sat here all the afternoon, watching her busy fingers send
That needle in and out. How soon, I wonder, will she reach the end?
Embroidery! I can't see how a girl of Molly's common sense
Can spend her time like that. Why, now—just look at that! I may be
    dense,
But, somehow, I don't see the fun in punching lots of holes down
    through
A piece of cloth; and, one by one, sewing them up. But Molly'll do

A dozen of them, right around
That shapeless bit of stuff she's found.

Appendices

A dozen of them! Just like that!
And think it's sense she's working at.

But then, she's just a girl (although she's quite the best one of the
    lot!),
And I'll just have to let her sew, whether it's foolishness or not.

II

(She)

He's sat here all the afternoon, talking about an awful game;
One boy will not be out till June, and then he may be always lame.
Foot-ball! I'm sure I can't see why a boy like Bob—so good and
    kind—
Wishes to see poor fellows lie hurt on the ground. I may be blind,
But, somehow, I don't see the fun. Some one calls, "14-16-9";
You kick the ball, and then you run and try to reach a white chalk-
    line.

And Bob would sit right there all day
And talk like that, and never say
A single word of sense; or so
It seems to me. I may not know.

But Bob's a faithful friend to me. So let him talk that game detested,
And I will smile and seem to be most wonderfully interested!

E. VINCENT MILLAY

APPENDIX B

THE fact was seized upon and made much of at the time in certain newspapers, that the story which Miss Millay had heard in her childhood and which, suddenly called upon to confront Governor Fuller and plead for clemency for the condemned men, and entirely unprepared, she remembered and related to him, was a very garbled account of what actually had taken place. Marked copies of newspapers containing vitriolic and insulting editorials were mailed to her, as well as foul and abusive letters.

The following letter from Edmund Pearson in the New York *World* of Thursday, August 25, 1927, page 10, is one of the first of many that pointed out the errors in the story. Miss Millay's excellent reply appeared in the same paper on October 6, 1927, page 12.

To the Editor of The World:

In today's papers, in the accounts of the execution of Sacco and Vanzetti, is this item:

"After Miss Millay was released she had an audience with Gov. Fuller. In about ten minutes she emerged and went to the Citizens' National Committee for Sacco and Vanzetti, where she dictated the following statement:

" 'This is the story of the last hanging in the state of Maine. This is the story I told Gov. Fuller. Two men were accused of having committed a murder. The evidence against them was very strong. It was so strong as to seem incontrovertible. On the side of the defense was only the testimony of a simple fisherman. This testimony, in the opinion of many persons, constituted a reasonable doubt, but in the mind of the Governor of Maine there was no doubt. The Governor did not believe that the fisherman told the truth. And the two men were hanged.

" 'Some time later, on his death-bed, the man who had committed the murder confessed. This was the last hanging in the state of Maine. In Maine to-day there is imprisonment for life. There is no more capital punishment.'

Appendices

"Miss Millay was asked how the Governor of Massachusetts received her story of Maine.

" 'He listened very politely,' she said, 'and he said he had never heard that story before.' "

In this story with which Miss Edna St. Vincent Millay saw fit to detain the Governor there is hardly any semblance of fact. The truth (which can be discovered in the Bar Association Library and in Edward P. Mitchell's "Memoirs of an Editor," page 106) is this:

The last execution of the death sentence in Maine was on June 25, 1875. Two men were executed for two different murders. One, named Gordon, had butchered three persons with an ax. There was never any doubt and never any dispute as to his guilt. The other, named Wagner, had killed two women, and also with an ax, at another time and place. He was seen and recognized and called by name by one of them before she died, and also seen and fully recognized by a third woman, who escaped alive and testified in court. The only man in the case to whom the term "simple fisherman" applies was the wretched husband of one of the women who came home and found the naked and murdered body of his young wife where the murderer, Wagner, had dragged it. Wagner had sat down and eaten supper beside it.

In prison Wagner became very pious, protested his innocence and tried to lay the blame for the murders on the sisters of one of his victims, a gentle Norwegian. He had hunted her and tried to kill her as well. His guilt was fully established and he was justly hanged. The truth about it has been told by a writer as distinguished in her day as Miss Millay in ours, and one not less humane, Celia Thaxter (Atlantic Monthly, May, 1875). Mrs. Thaxter who lived within sight of the murders and knew all the participants, had no doubt of Wagner's guilt and resented the foul slander on an innocent woman.

Wagner's religious hypocrisy foiled a few people for a while. Years afterwards an absurd yarn arose about a death-bed confession by the surviving woman. It has never received the slightest credence by anybody not ignorant of the facts. Miss Millay's story, which she added to Gov. Fuller's somewhat burdened day, is a still further garbled version of this old slander.

EDMUND PEARSON

New York, Aug. 23.

Mr. Pearson's own errors Miss Millay points out in the following letter.

Edna St. Vincent Millay

To the Editor of The World:

Some time ago Mr. Edmund Pearson in a letter to your paper pointed out that in an interview granted me by the Governor of Massachusetts on the afternoon before the execution of Sacco and Vanzetti, I told, as being true, a story which had little foundation in reality. It happened that Mr. Pearson had recently been engaged in writing a book about the very episode which I had in mind and had gone to some trouble to look up the facts. My story was inaccurate in almost every detail.

When I was a child I had heard from several people accounts of the murders on the Isle of Shoals and of the hanging of Louis Wagner in the State Prison of Thomaston. These people all believed Wagner to have been innocent. Fishermen and longshoremen had testified, it seems, that no man could row out to the Isle of Shoals and back, a distance of twenty miles, in the time for which Wagner was unable to present an alibi. After the execution it seemed somebody had confessed, and in horror at having committed so tragic an error the State of Maine abolished capital punishment. There are many people in Maine to-day who still believe that Wagner was innocent. "I was not in Portsmouth an hour," writes Mr. Pearson in his book on the subject, "nor on the Isle of Shoals half an hour before I heard repeated the doubts of his guilt."

When I spoke with Gov. Fuller I had not heard the tale in twenty years. The story, inaccurate in itself apparently, I remembered inaccurately. I recalled that Wagner and another man had been executed at the same time. I construed it as having been for the same murder. The story is that a woman confessed. I remembered it as having been a man. What I clearly recalled was that in Maine somebody had been hanged for murder, had subsequently been found to be innocent, and that on account of this capital punishment had been abolished in that state. "This," I said to Gov. Fuller, "is the story I heard when I was a child." I firmly believed it to be the truth. I was mistaken.

In his letter to The World Mr. Pearson, who, as I have said, had recently gone to some trouble to look up the facts, makes the following statement: "The last execution of the death sentence in Maine was on June 25, 1875"; that is to say, the execution of Gordon and Wagner. Mr. Pearson is mistaken.

Mr. E. P. Mitchell, who had followed the Wagner case faithfully and had been present at the execution, says in his "Memoirs of an Editor," "That was the last capital execution in Maine." Mr. Mitchell is mistaken.

Mr. Fred K. Owen in the Portland (Me.) Sunday Telegram of

Appendices

Sept. 25 discusses my mistake. He also points out to Mr. Pearson his mistake, and to Mr. Mitchell his: The last execution of the death sentence in Maine was the hanging of Daniel Wilkinson, Nov. 20, 1885.

Mr. Owen goes on to say: "Mr. Mitchell (in his "Memoirs") states that he talked with Wagner the night before the execution and had no doubt of his guilt." I quote now from Mr. Mitchell's "Memoirs": "When I left the cell that night after seeing how the condemned bore himself and hearing his simple, forcible discussion of the case, there was doubt and not certainty in my mind." Mr. Owen is mistaken.

Mr. Owen further says: "During those twelve years (that is, between the execution of Gordon and Wagner in 1875 and the abolition of the death penalty in 1887) there had been but one execution of a murderer, and that was in 1885, when Daniel Wilkinson of Bath was hanged." But in a letter to the Rockland Courier-Gazette, dated Sept. 26, Mr. Oscar Blunt of Thomaston writes: "I have a correct record of the hangings," and goes on to give a list of them concluding with "Gordon and Wagner, June 24, 1875; Capone and Santore, Italians, April 17, 1885; and Daniel Wilkinson, Nov. 20, 1885." Again, somebody is mistaken.

Sir, on the afternoon before the execution of Sacco and Vanzetti I sought an interview with Gov. Fuller because I believed that the Governor was about to make a serious mistake. I understood that he had gone carefully into the evidence and that he believed the two men to be guilty. But I questioned him: In a case where the lives of two men depended upon his decision, and where so many thoughtful citizens, although not in sympathy with the political opinions of these men, nevertheless were convinced that they had been unfairly tried, could he be so sure of his own judgment as to go forward with these executions in the face of the knowledge that human beings often err? As an illustration of the fallibility of the human mind I told him the story as I remembered it, of an instance of the grave miscarriage of justice in a neighboring State. If in the very illustration which I used I was myself in error the force of my assertion is not lessened—that human beings with the best intentions in the world often made mistakes.

Gov. Fuller, secure in his own mind against the pleadings of myself and of many other persons more eloquent and more qualified to speak, refused to intervene for Sacco and Vanzetti. That Gov. Fuller himself made a mistake is very far from impossible.

EDNA ST. VINCENT MILLAY

Austerlitz, N. Y. Oct. 4.

FOREWORD TO THE
BIBLIOGRAPHY

I have been asked to write a foreword to this bibliography, a work whose good fortune I truly desire, but the nature of whose value or interest to anybody I do not understand. As for myself, I am a collector of sea-shells. I live in the strong though ebbing hope of finding someday on a briefly uncovered sand-bar a right-handed Left-Handed Whelk; or even, someday, after propitious foul weather, of digging out of the beach under the jealous eyes of hundreds who dare not quite attack me and wrest it from me, a perfect Junonia. The very thought of the words *"Conus gloria-maris, Hwass"* fills me with an ecstasy of longing and despair. But the sight of the words "matchless copy of Hookes' *Amanda*, with both blank leaves G5 and H" leaves me unaffected. However, as I said, to this bibliography, and to its compiler and to its readers, I wish good fortune. As a maniac in one department, I salute the maniacs in another: may sweet Insanity forever charm our days.

EDNA ST. VINCENT MILLAY

Steepletop
February, 1937

[67]

PREFACE

THIS preface will deal largely with assertions made in the bibliography, but not with the propriety of the issuance of a bibliography of a living author. That old discussion has no attraction for me, and I do not wish or propose to reopen it here, regardless of the excellent opportunity I would have because of the obvious merit of my position. It seems to me to be unnecessary to argue the subject when a living author enjoys the hold on the reading and collecting public that Edna St. Vincent Millay does. Since her first book, her succeeding volumes have been the cause of eager inquiry on the part of book buyers throughout the country, and subsequent to their appearance there has been a steady demand necessitating the reprinting of certain volumes many times.

Earnest readers of this bibliography will perceive the intricacies of many publications. The first volume given a full collation was issued in 1912. The volumes which gave me the most difficulty were issued between 1920 and 1922. Even the latter year is sufficiently long passed to subject the statements of anyone speaking of those years, to severe scrutiny. The task would not attenuate by postponement, and the fallibility of memory is best removed from the reckoning as soon as possible. I cannot see why we should court the additional possibility of error or at least uncertainty by requiring that the demise of the author precede any thorough research into the author's works.

Publication of a bibliography at this time does not imply that Miss Millay's activity has ceased. On the contrary, for the purpose of encompassing the future works in the same volume there are provided a few blank pages for future collations.

I make the usual untrue declaration of bibliographers, that I shall be glad to have called to my attention any errors, omissions, or discoveries. The truth is that I shall be chagrined, annoyed, or displeased, depending on the nature of the complaint. If the reader has reason to believe that I have erred, as a courtesy to the dealers and to the collecting fraternity I ask that he correspond with me, before making a conflicting pronouncement on a point which I might have investigated and discarded.

Usages peculiar to this bibliography are explained here. Although they may not conform to all other bibliographies, they are uniform throughout this book, and this key will be of some assistance.

In the section devoted to criticisms I have included parodies and dedications. I could not overlook them, and they are hardly so numerous that they deserve a separate section. They are a form of criticism because they evince a conscious regard of the subject.

When, in describing the appearance of a title-page, I say that certain lines are in a certain type, I refer to, and count, lines of printing, exclusive of seals or rules or illustrations. Any words in italic in the collations indicate that the exact words appearing on the particular page are quoted, but without regard to the type in which those words are set in the book collated.

In the descriptions of covers and backbones the use of small capitals indicates that the lettering is die-stamped; the use of upper and lower case indicates that the lettering is printed.

The phrase "Copies deposited", means deposited in the Library of Congress to secure copyright. The terms 4to,

Preface

8vo, 12mo, etc., refer to the folding of the signatures, and not to the page size, which is given in inches.

Separate attention is given to each different collation regardless of whether that collation is of a book which is not a first printing by reason of the material it contains. This is done in order to aid the novice and also the dealers who are often approached by wishful vendors of what appears to the unpractised eye to be a first edition. Harper & Brothers first editions, and English first editions, for instance, are thus included. I have included also a dummy of one book (*Twice Required*), and considered its contents as a first printing, and have not included other dummies, because the title of the collated dummy was changed before publication. This is a unique case.

Some question may be raised by my including *The Lyric Year* among the full collations. It is a pertinent and valuable book, and it has an interesting history. Contrarily, however, I did not include full collations of the important anthologies containing one or more first book printings of poems, nor of the anthologies containing one of the plays. One must draw the line somewhere, and the various appearances of the play are mentioned in the collations of its separate appearances.

For the benefit of the student of modern American poetry I have included, or tried to include, all periodical appearances, and not merely first appearances. This affords an opportunity to see what editors consider are the best poems, or the poems with the most popular or specialized class appeal. For the same reason I have given the list of poems in the English *Poems* and in *Poems Selected for Young People*, although there is only one first printing in the former and none in the latter: the selections were made by Miss Millay and again might aid the student.

I now come to the most pleasant task of all, that of

Edna St. Vincent Millay

expressing my thanks to book people who have helped me. Foremost among these is my dear friend John Kohn, the New York dealer, whose response to my original announcement in 1932 was the basis of a valued friendship. Through his indefatigable efforts I have acquired information that otherwise I should never have had. His voluminous and thorough correspondence provides the most personal record I possess of my work on this book; his altruism concerning his many discoveries has served to strengthen my realization of the position I hold with reference to persons dependent on this book for reliable guidance.

I am indebted to Miss Harriet Monroe of the magazine *Poetry*, and to Mr. Charles H. Tenney of New York, for the privilege of examining their collections. Mr. Tenney possesses the finest collection of Millay material that I know of, and he placed it at my disposal on several occasions, thus greatly facilitating comparisons.

Three other dealers have helped me generously. I refer to R. J. Barry of New Haven, David A. Randall of New York, and John G. Kidd of Cincinnati, all of whom have been quick to respond to my requests. Harold Lewis Cook, whose illuminating essay forms part of this book, Frank Shay, now a literary agent in New York, who was responsible for numerous publications whose importance today indicate his judgment, John G. Neihardt, the literary editor of the St. Louis *Post-Dispatch*, Martin Secker, Frederick W. Goudy, all have my thanks. Those booksellers in Chicago and New York who have tolerated my inspecting their stocks (usually without buying), in the last few years, will by this statement know that they are included in my appreciation.

Wilmette, Illinois
January, 1937   KARL YOST

BIBLIOGRAPHY

SECTION I
COLLATIONS

BIBLIOGRAPHY

1.   THE LYRIC YEAR: 1912

The | Lyric Year | One Hundred Poems | Edited by | Ferdinand Earle | [*publisher's monogram*] | New York | Mitchell Kennerley | 1912
   Title-page in capitals throughout.

Collation: Pp. xii + 320, consisting of, after white endsheet, and two blank leaves not counted in pagination; p.[i] title-page as above (copyright on verso) ; pp. iii-v, *The Lyric Year Prizes*; p.[vi] blank; pp. vii-viii, *Note by the Editor*; pp.[ix-xii], *The Lyric Year* (table of contents) ; pp. 1-298, text; pp. 299-316, *Lyric Year Contributors*; pp.[317-320] blank; endsheet.

8vo, size 5 x 7⅜. Bound in maroon cloth, figure of lyre gold-stamped in center of front cover, three-rule border blind-stamped around edges. Backbone lettered in gold, first three lines in capitals, last two in upper and lower case: [*three blind rules*] | THE | LYRIC | YEAR | MITCHELL | KENNERLEY | [*three blind rules*]. Gilt top. Fore and lower edges rough trimmed.

There are three issues of this book, all bearing the same date on the title-page. The first issue measures one inch across the top, including covers; page 41, line 4, reads "When star meets star"; and there is a monogram blind-stamped on the back cover. The second issue was printed on heavier paper than the first, and measures 1 3/32 inches across the top, including covers; page 41, line 4, reads "When star meets crystal star"; there is a monogram blind-stamped on the back cover; and there are no blank leaves at the end. The third issue is like the second except that there is no monogram on the back cover.

I have taken only one textual mutation (page 41, line 4) from the many suggested by Mr. Nelson F. Adkins in his extensive article on

Edna St. Vincent Millay

The Lyric Year, which appeared in *The American Book Collector* for March, 1933, vol. III, no. 3, p. 148. I use the above material through the kind permission of Mr. Adkins, and of Mr. Charles F. Heartman, the editor, and I refer interested persons to the article for complete explanation of the points.

The backbone of the dust-wrapper of the first issue has the date (1912) in parentheses. The backbones of the dust-wrappers of the second and third issues do not have the date at all. I state this merely as a matter of record.

The first appearance in print of "Renascence" by Edna St. Vincent Millay is on pp. 180-188. This poem was one of thousands submitted in a prize competition sponsored by Mr. Earle, who selected one hundred poems (the entire selection published as *The Lyric Year*) from which the prize winners were chosen. Although Mr. Earle, himself a judge, voted to award the first prize to "Renascence", neither Mr. William Stanley Braithwaite nor Mr. Edward J. Wheeler, the other judges, mentioned it in their ballots, and Miss Millay did not receive a prize. Jessie B. Rittenhouse, in *My House of Life* (cf. Section II), makes pertinent comment on this subject.

The Lyric Year has become a desirable item not only because it is the earliest anthology called forth by the contemporary poetry revival, but also because it contains the first appearance of Miss Millay's masterful poem. I place it first among the collations in order to give it bibliographical recognition commensurate with its literary importance.

2. BACCALAUREATE HYMN: 1917

Commencement Week | Vassar College | June Ninth | to | June Twelfth | Nineteen hundred and seventeen
   All the above in capitals.

Collation: Pp.[18], unnumbered throughout, consisting of title-page as above (verso blank); program of the week (verso blank); program of the week—continued (verso blank); Baccalaureate Sunday (verso blank); Baccalaureate Hymn (verso blank); Class Day (verso blank); Class Day

[76]

Bibliography

—continued (verso blank) ; Commencement day (verso blank) ; Class Officers (verso blank).

Size $4\frac{9}{16}$ x $5\frac{13}{16}$. Parchment with purple leather thong tie. Date 1917 within an owl embossed in purple, and embossed border on front cover. Back cover blank. Tissue guard between covers and text.

The Baccalaureate Hymn is signed at the bottom of the page in italic, *Edna St. Vincent Millay, 1917*. This is the regular commencement announcement prepared for and sold to the members of the graduating class, as is the custom in almost all colleges.

2A.   BROADSIDE

Subsequent to the printing of the foregoing item a broadside of the Baccalaureate Hymn separately was printed for the use of the class in rehearsing the piece prior to its presentation at the services on Baccalaureate Sunday. This broadside, measuring $5\frac{1}{4}$ x $8\frac{13}{16}$, was printed from the plate used for the page bearing the Hymn in the program for the Baccalaureate Services (cf. Collation No. 2B), and is identical therewith except that the words "Baccalaureate Hymn" were removed from the upper left corner. Despite the fact that it was printed from the same plate, it was distributed before the programs were distributed, and thereby takes precedence. This broadside is the first separate printing of any work by Miss Millay and needless to say, because of its fragile character, and its purpose, is quite rare. I have seen only one copy of it. (See Cut A.)

2B.   PROGRAM

Vassar College | Baccalaureate Service | in the chapel | at 10 o'clock a.m. | June 10, 1917
All the above in Old English type.

8 unnumbered pages. Baccalaureate Hymn on p.[5] together with the music, headed as follows: Baccalaureate

Tune:—"St. Vincent."

Words and music by EDNA ST. VINCENT MILLAY, '17.

1. Thou great of-fend-ed God of love and kind-ness,
2. Bright are the ban-ners on the tents of laugh-ter;
3. Dark were the ways where of our-selves we sought Thee,
4. Since we are dust, how shall we not be-tray Thee?
5. "Lord, Lord!" we cried of old, who now be-fore Thee,

We have de-nied, we have for-got-ten Thee!
Shunned is Thy tem-ple,—weeds are on the path,
An-guish, De-ris-ion, Doubt, De-sire and Mirth;
Still blows a-bout the world the an-cient wind—
Strick-en with prayer, shak-en with praise, are dumb;

With deaf-er sense en-dow, en-light-en us with blind-ness,
Yet if Thou leave us, Lord, what help is ours there-aft-er?—
Twist-ed, ob-scure, un-love-ly, Lord, the gifts we brought Thee,
Nor yet for lives un-tried and tear-less would we pray Thee:
Fa-ther ac-cept our wor-ship when we least a-dore Thee,

Who, hav-ing ears and eyes, nor hear nor see.
Be with us still,—light not to-day Thy wrath!
Teach us what ways have light, what gifts have worth.
Lord let us suf-fer that we may grow kind!
And when we call Thee not, oh, hear and come!

CUT A. BACCALAUREATE HYMN BROADSIDE

Bibliography

Hymn: | Tune:—"St. Vincent". | Words and music by Edna St. Vincent Millay, '17. The author's name is in caps and small caps. Size $6\frac{1}{16}$ x $9\frac{5}{16}$. Printed on paper watermarked U.S.A. Blandford Book. White silk tie.

This is the only one of the three forms of the hymn bearing an exact date, but I believe I have arrived at their correct order. The latter two forms carry both words and music; the first carries the words alone.

3. RENASCENCE AND OTHER POEMS: 1917

Renascence | and | Other Poems | by | Edna St. Vincent Millay | [*publisher's monogram*] | New York | Mitchell Kennerley | MCMXVII
  Title-page in capitals throughout.

Collation: Pp. x + 78, consisting of, after endsheet; pp.[I-IV] blank; p.[V] bastard title (verso blank); p.[VII] title-page as above (copyright on verso); p.[IX] contents list (verso blank); pp. 1-73, text; pp.[74-78]; blank; endsheet.

12mo, size 5 x $7\frac{5}{8}$. Bound in black ribbed cloth. *Renascence* on front cover in gold capitals. Backbone lettered in gold capitals: RENASCENCE | EDNA | ST. VINCENT | MILLAY | MITCHELL | KENNERLEY. Back cover blank. All edges uncut.

Published December 17, 1917. Copies deposited December 26, 1917. The first edition was printed, after cutting, on sheets watermarked *AGM Glaslan* in the center and (*France*) in the lower right corner. The second edition was printed, after cutting, on sheets watermarked *MBM* along the top edge and *MBM* (*France*) *Ingres d'Arches* along the bottom edge. However, it is possible that there are copies of the first edition which, due to the manner in which the sheets were folded and cut, do not show any watermark. Further, I know that no watermark *Ingres d'Arches* will be found on any copies of the second edition, because the portion of the sheet bearing that part of the watermark was trimmed off; this was about 4¼ inches. Watermarks alone do not provide an infallible guide to distinction between the first and second editions. I have found that because of the difference in the size of the sheets used in the two editions, the signatures of the two were not formed alike, and a difference in the collations is the result: the second edition has eight fewer pages than the first. This difference, together with typographical changes, is set forth in the following schedule.

Two blank leaves, exclusive of end-paper preceding bastard-title in first; no blank leaves preceding bastard-title in second.

Two blank leaves, exclusive of end-paper, following p. (74) in first; no blank leaves following p. (74) in second.

Semicolon at end of penultimate line on p. 1 of first; colon at end of penultimate line on p. 1 of second.

Period at end of sixth line from bottom on p. 37 of first; no period at end of same line of second.

Comma at end of first line on p. 70 of first; period at end of same line of second.

The changes in punctuation made in the second edition were retained throughout later printings by Kennerley and by Harper & Brothers.

LIMITED EDITION

Simultaneously with the first edition there were printed fifteen copies on Japan vellum, having the same title-page and collation as the regular edition. These were all signed by the author. On p. (74) is this note: This is number (number in ink) of fifteen copies printed on Japan vellum.

Contents, first book printing for all poems except those marked with asterisk:
* Renascence
* Interim
* The Suicide
* God's World
  Afternoon on a Hill
  Sorrow
  Tavern
* Ashes of Life
  The Little Ghost

Bibliography

Kin to Sorrow
Three Songs of Shattering
* The Shroud
The Dream
Indifference
Witch-wife
Blight
When the year grows old

Unnamed Sonnets I-V
Thou art not lovelier than lilacs—no
Time does not bring relief; you all have lied
Mindful of you the sodden earth in spring
Not in this chamber only at my birth
If I should learn, in some quite casual way
Sonnet VI [Bluebeard] This door you might not open and you did

4. ARIA DA CAPO, Chapbook: 1920

Aria da Capo | (A Play in One Act) | By | Edna St. Vincent Millay | The Chapbook | (A Monthly Miscellany) | No. 14. August 1920

Second and sixth lines (which are in parentheses) and the word "No." in upper and lower case; all rest in capitals.

Collation: Pp. II + 24 + II, consisting of pp.[I-II], advertisements; p.[1] title-page as above (production notice on verso); pp. 3-24, text; pp. III-[IV], advertisements.

Square 8vo, size 6⅝ x 8½. Binding of pictorial wrappers, designed by Albert Rutherston. Front wrapper: The Chapbook | No 14 | [A Monthly Miscellany] August 1920 | [*rule*] | [*illustration in black and two colors*] | [*rule*] | Aria da Capo By | [A Play in One Act] Edna St. Vincent Millay | [*two rules*]. The foregoing is set within a single rule border. Outside the border in the lower right corner is: One Shilling and Sixpence Net. Back wrapper has a colored vignette in the center. Insides of front and back wrappers carry advertisements. Top and fore edges trimmed; lower edge uncut.

Edna St. Vincent Millay

First separate publication of this play, which was printed first in *Reedy's Mirror* for March 18, 1920. I give this present periodical printing a full collation because it occupies the entire number, and because I am pleased to echo Miss Harriet Monroe's statement that this is the biggest piece Miss Millay ever wrote.

On p.(2) there is a list of little theatre groups which had produced *Aria da Capo*, viz.: Provincetown Players' Theatre, New York City, Boston Community Players, Boston, Vagabond Theatre, Baltimore, and The Little Theatre, St. Louis. It was also translated into French and played in Paris, I understand. None of the scripts used by any of these groups has been brought to my attention; it may be that some or all of them were printed, and constitute printings earlier than that of the present collation.

5. A FEW FIGS FROM THISTLES: 1920

A Few Figs | From Thistles | [*three small square boxes*] | Poems and Four Sonnets | By Edna St. Vincent Millay | [*three small square boxes*] | [*line drawing of seated nude figure, within semi-circle*] | Salvo: Published by Frank Shay | Four Christopher Street, New York | 1920

All the above is in capitals except the words "By", "Published by", and "Four Christopher Street, New York", which are upper and lower case.

Collation: Pp. 20, consisting of p.[1] bastard title (advertisement on verso) ; p.[3] title-page as above (contents list on verso) ; pp. 5-18, text; pp. 19-20, advertisements.

8vo, size of leaf 6⅜ x 8⅛; size of wrapper varies around 6½ x 8¼. Wrappers printed in black ink in upper right corner, in capitals except last word: Salvo One | A Few Figs [*two devices*] | From Thistles | Poems and Four Sonnets By | Edna St. Vincent Millay | [*line drawing as on title-page*] | Frank Shay [*two devices*] Publisher 1920. Back wrapper blank. All edges trimmed.

Bibliography

This, the first edition of *A Few Figs From Thistles*, was issued in red, lemon yellow, orange, electric blue, purple, and green wrappers. All wrappers of the first five colors and some of the green have (or had at one time) a folded-over flap which has often been described as a "wallet edge". Neither the color of the wrappers nor the presence of the flap is a point of issue.

Sometime about the end of September, 1920, Frank Shay ordered 1000 copies printed. With the intention of making a vivid window display in his shop at 4 Christopher Street, New York City, he bought from the Japan Paper Company five sheets each of red, lemon yellow, orange, electric blue, and purple paper. From each sheet he was able to make two wrappers. He bought green paper for wrappers on the rest of the edition. On a Saturday morning the printer finished the run, but because the trimmer in the printing shop had left for the day, the first shipment, being all of the bright colors (50 in all, 10 of each) and about 150 of the green, was delivered to Frank Shay's shop with the back wrapper projecting about 2¾ inches beyond the fore-edge of the text. To save time, Mr. Shay merely folded over these projecting portions, forming the flap or wallet edge. The window was filled with the five bright colors, and the green wrapper copies were stacked inside, to be given to customers who had been attracted by the colors. On the following Monday the remaining 800 copies in green wrappers were delivered with all edges of the wrappers properly trimmed.

All the sheets were printed in a single run. It is impossible to say which sheets were bound first. Copies in green, with or without flap, were probably sold first. On the basis of the foregoing data, which I have from Frank Shay, I repeat that color has nothing to do with priority, although the five enumerated colors are scarcer, and the flap has nothing to do with priority. Furthermore, this flap easily dropped off at the fold, and left an edge that cannot be told from a worn edge that had once been trimmed.

I can give no more accurate publication date than the latter part of September, 1920. There are no copies in the Library of Congress.

Contents, first book printing for all poems except that marked with asterisk:
First Fig
Second Fig

[83]

Thursday
The Penitent
The Unexplorer
* She is Overheard Singing
The Merry Maid
Portrait by a Neighbor
The Philosopher
To the Not Impossible Him
Daphne
Sonnet—Love Though For This
Sonnet—I Think I Should Have Loved You
Sonnet—Oh. Think Not I am Faithful
Sonnet—I Shall Forget You Presently

6. A FEW FIGS FROM THISTLES:
1921

A Few Figs From Thistles | [*double rule*] | Poems and Four Sonnets By | Edna St. Vincent Millay | [*publisher's monogram*] | Salvo: Published by Frank Shay | Four Christopher Street, New York City | 1921

Fifth line, and words "Published by" are in upper and lower case; rest in capitals.

Collation: Pp. 16, consisting of p.[1] title-page as above (contents list and acknowledgments on verso); pp. 3-16, text.

8vo, size of leaf $6\frac{11}{16}$ x $8\frac{5}{16}$, of wrapper $7\frac{3}{16}$ x 9. Binding of green wrappers, bearing on front cover printing as on the title-page, except for the date, enclosed in $\frac{3}{32}$-inch border. Back cover bears an announcement of *The Measure*, with the names of all the contributing editors. Insides of front and back covers bear advertisements.

This edition, which contains the same material as the first edition of 1920 (cf. Collation No. 5), was issued in March, 1921, to supply the demand which had exhausted the earlier edition. Mr. Shay told me that he thought of this as the "Gashouse Edition" (I believe because it was a pot-boiler), and that he sold several thousand copies of it.

7. A FEW FIGS FROM THISTLES, Enlarged: 1921

A Few Figs From Thistles | Poems and Sonnets | By Edna St. Vincent Millay | [*publisher's monogram in rectangle*] | New and Enlarged Edition | Frank Shay | New York | 1921
Second, fourth, and sixth lines, and word "By" in upper and lower case; rest in capitals. Fourth line in italic.

Collation: Pp. 32, consisting of; pp.[1-2] blank; p.[3] bastard title (list of books on verso) ; p.[5] title-page as above (copyright on verso) ; p.[7] half-title; p. 8 contents list; pp. 9-28, text; pp.[29-32] blank.

8vo, size 5 x 7¼. The first edition appeared in two styles of wrappers; they are described in order of precedence.

1. Leaf green wrappers, pasted over heavy art paper, about two inches being folded over. Front wrapper bears two boxes made by reversed color woodblock with darker green ink. Upper box: A Few | Figs | From | Thistles. Lower box: Edna | St Vincent | Millay. Back wrapper bears a box in lower right corner: Frank Shay's | Book Shop · · 4 Christopher St. N. Y. All lettering is in capitals. All edges trimmed.

2. Jade green wrappers, pasted over heavy art paper, no part being folded over. Front wrapper: By Edna St. Vincent Millay | [*staggered rule*] | A Few Figs from Thistles | Poems and Sonnets | [*staggered rule*] | New York Frank Shay Publisher. The foregoing is in black across the top. Proper names are in capitals, rest upper and lower case; the third line in italic.

The first wrapper was printed from linoleum blocks cut by a friend of Frank Shay, before the completion of the printing of the second wrapper. The pages of the foregoing different issues are alike.

Subsequent editions have on the title-page: New York | Frank Shay | 1921, that is, "New York" precedes "Frank Shay" and is in upper and lower case. Also, in subsequent editions, the name of the book by Miss Millay listed on the verso of the bastard title as "In Preparation" is "Child Songs", not "Little Acorns". Exactly how many printings there were I do not know, but I have seen galley proofs labeled in the hand of a contemporary proof-reader, "5th edn".

First issued in late June or early July, 1921. Although there is a copyright notice on the verso of the title-page, this book was not registered for copyright. The copy in the Library of Congress was purchased some time after publication.

Contents: in addition to the fifteen poems of the 1920 edition (cf. Collation No. 5), this contains the following new poems, herein first printed.

To S. M.
The Singing Woman From the Wood's Edge
Grown-up
The Prisoner

The poems "To S. M." and "Thursday" are listed in that order in the list of contents on p. 8, but are transposed in the text. This transposition appears in all copies I have examined, and apparently does not constitute a point of issue.

8.   THE LAMP AND THE BELL:
1921

The Lamp | and the Bell | A Drama in Five Acts | By Edna St. Vincent Millay | New York | Frank Shay | 1921
All the above in capitals, except third line and the word "by" which are in upper and lower case italic.

Collation: Pp. 72, consisting of p.[1] bastard title (list of books in box on verso); p.[3] title-page as above (copyright on verso); pp. 5-6 dramatis personae; pp. 7-71, text; p.[72] blank.

12mo, size 5 x 8. There were three printings of this book, each issued in a different binding, listed below in their order

Bibliography

of precedence according to notes and recollections of Mr. Shay. I am unable to give the exact date of publication of any of the three, but Mr. Shay says the first printing was coetaneous with the printing of the first enlarged edition of *A Few Figs* (cf. Collation No. 7). There are no copies in the Library of Congress, the earliest record of *The Lamp and the Bell* there being an entry in September 1922 (cf. Collation No. 12). The three printings differ in many small typographical particulars, but the bindings provide sufficient identification.

1. Green wrappers, all edges overlapping the text, lettered in black across the top of the front cover, the author's and publisher's names in capitals, the third line in italic upper and lower case, and the rest in roman upper and lower case: By Edna St. Vincent Millay | [*rule*] | The Lamp and The Bell | A Drama in Five Acts | [*rule*] | New York Frank Shay Publisher. Backbone lettered in Hobo type, reading from bottom to top, the author's name in capitals: Edna St. Vincent Millay: The Lamp and The Bell. All edges trimmed. This was listed in the weekly record of *Publishers' Weekly* for July 23, 1921. The books listed on the verso of the half-title are *A Few Figs, Aria da Capo*, and *Renascence*.

2. Orange wrappers, lettered on front cover, the third and fourth lines in italic upper and lower case, the word "and" in lower case, and the remaining four words of the title in capitals: The Lamp | and The Bell | A Drama in Five Acts | By Edna St. Vincent Millay. In the lower right corner of the front cover there is printed from a linoleum or wood block, in capitals: Frank | Shay's | Bookshop. The list of books on the verso of the half-title is the same as in (1.) above.

3. Black boards of a smooth, dull finish. Covers blank. 16mo, size 5¼ x 7⅞. Backbone lettered in gold capitals: THE | LAMP | AND THE | BELL | EDNA | ST · V · | MILLAY | FRANK | SHAY. All edges trimmed. The list of books on the verso of the half-title has added to it *Two Slatterns* and *Second April*. The former having been published November 5, 1921, it is possible to date this edition, roughly.

Edna St. Vincent Millay

This play was written in Paris, and produced outdoors at Vassar College sometime in June of 1921. Mr. Shay told me that the first printing was put out in great haste so that it might reach Poughkeepsie in time for the presentation. The play was written for the 50th anniversary of the founding of the Vassar College Alumnae Association.

9.   SECOND APRIL: 1921

Second April | Edna St. Vincent Millay | ·[*publisher's monogram*] | New York | Mitchell Kennerley | MCMXXI
Title-page in capitals throughout.

Collation: Pp. VIII + 112, consisting of, after endsheet; p.[I] bastard title (list of books on verso) ; p.[III] title-page as above (copyright on verso) ; p.[V] dedication (verso blank) ; p.[VII] contents list (verso blank) ; pp.[1]-112, text; endsheet.

12mo, size 4⅞ x 7½. Bound in black ribbed cloth. *Second April* gold stamped on front cover in capitals. Backbone lettered in gold capitals: SECOND | APRIL | EDNA | ST. VINCENT | MILLAY | MITCHELL | KENNERLEY. Back cover blank. All edges uncut.

Published August 4, 1921. Copies deposited August 25, 1921. The first edition is printed on Glaslan paper, similar to that used in the first edition of *Renascence* (cf. Collation No. 3). Although the signatures were folded alike in the two books, the necessity of identification through watermarks is obviated because the second edition of *Second April*, which was printed in September 1921, on Deckle d'Aigle paper, carries a record of the printing on the verso of the title-page. The third and successive editions were printed on Alexandra and other papers, and the verso of the title-page of each edition carries the record of the printing.

Contents: (First book printing except for those poems marked with an asterisk.)
Spring
City Trees

Bibliography

And you as well must die, beloved dust
Let you not say of me when I am old
Oh, my beloved, have you thought of this:
As to some lovely temple, tenantless
Cherish you then the hope I shall forget
* Wild Swans

10. TWO SLATTERNS AND A KING: 1921

Two Slatterns and | a King | A Moral Interlude | By |
Edna St. Vincent Millay | Author of "Aria da Capo",
etc. | First produced at Vassar College | [*publishers' seal*] |
Cincinnati | Stewart Kidd Company | Publishers

*There is no date on the title-page. All the above in capitals
except fourth, sixth and seventh lines, which are in upper
and lower case.*

Collation: Pp. 20, consisting of p.[1] bastard title (advertisement on verso) ; p.[3] title-page as above (verso: *Copyright
1921*) ; p.[5] dramatis personae (verso blank) ; p.[7] note on
prologue (verso blank) ; pp. 9-18, text; pp.[19-20] advertisements.

8vo, size 4⅝ x 7¾. Binding of heavy art paper wrappers; on
each side of front cover, running the length of the cover, are
three vertical bars in green. In the center between the two
sets of bars, there is printing, in capitals as follows: Two | Slat-
terns | and a | King | By | Edna St. Vincent | Millay | [*vignette
of masques in green intaglio*] | Stewart Kidd | Modern Plays |
Edited by | Frank Shay. The verso of the front cover, and
both sides of the back cover, carry advertisements. All edges
trimmed.

Published November 5, 1921. Copies deposited November 10, 1921.
Copyright January 16, 1920 as an unpublished play. The second
printing, in February 1924, is so marked on the title-page and on
the verso of the title-page.

Bibliography

11. ARIA DA CAPO: 1921

Aria da Capo | A Play in One Act | Edna St. Vincent
Millay | [*publisher's monogram in circle*] | New York |
Mitchell Kennerley | MCMXXI
Title-page in capitals throughout.

Collation: Pp. vi + 58, consisting of, after white endsheet;
pp.[i-iv] blank; p.[v] bastard title (list of books on verso);
p.[1] title-page as above (copyright on verso); p.[3] half-title
(*Persons* on verso); pp. 5-36, text of play; p.[37] *Author's Note*
(verso blank); p.[39] *Original cast* (verso blank); pp. 41-42,
Author's Note; pp. 43-55, suggestions for production; pp.[56-
58] blank; endsheet.

8vo, size 5⅛ x 7¹¹⁄₁₆. Bound in black cloth. Front cover lettered
in gold capitals: ARIA DA CAPO. Backbone lettered in gold capi-
tals: ARIA | DA | CAPO | EDNA | ST. VINCENT | MILLAY | MITCHELL
| KENNERLEY. Back cover blank. All edges untrimmed.

Published very late in December, 1921, or early in January, 1922.
There are no copies in the Library of Congress, but I have seen a
review copy stamped as received by the reviewer on January 5, 1922.

Issuance of copyright for the unpublished play the previous year,
on January 16, 1920, explains the discrepancy between the date on
the title-page (1921) and the date on the verso of the title-page
(1920). See index for relative position of this edition of the play.
The "Author's suggestions for the production of the play" are here
first published.

12. THE LAMP AND THE BELL,
Synthetic: 1922

The Lamp and the Bell | A Drama in Five Acts | [*rule*] |
By Edna St. Vincent Millay
*There is no date on the title-page. All the above in capitals,
except the word "by". Second line in italic.*

Collation: Pp. 68, consisting of; one blank leaf; title-page as above (copyright on verso) ; dramatis personae (continued on verso) ; pp.[272]-333, text; verso p. 333 blank; one blank leaf.

8vo, size   ?   . Binding of sand colored wrappers, bearing same printing as that on title-page. This is a synthetic volume. Parts of those two signatures from the book *A Treasury of Plays for Women* (published by Little, Brown & Co. on September 16, 1922) , which contained *The Lamp and the Bell* were stapled together and bound in a specially printed wrapper to make a separate issue of this one play. The title-page given above is the half-title to the play as it appears in *A Treasury of Plays for Women.* The only copy of this edition of which I am aware may be found, *mirabile dictu,* in the rare book room of the Library of Congress.

13. A FEW FIGS FROM THISTLES:
1922

A Few Figs From Thistles | Poems and Sonnets | By | Edna St. Vincent Millay | New and | enlarged edition | Frank Shay   Stewart Kidd | Publisher   Distributor | New York   Cincinnati

There is no date on the title-page. See cut.

Collation: Pp. 40, consisting of, after endsheet; p.[1] bastard title (list of books on verso) ; p.[3] title-page as above (verso: *Copyright 1922 by Frank Shay*) ; p.[5] half-title (acknowledgment note on verso) ; p. 7 contents list (verso blank) pp. 9-34, text; p. 35 *Four Sonnets*; pp. 36-39, text of Four Sonnets; p.[40] blank; endsheet.

8vo, size 5¼ x 7½. Green boards, black cloth back. Front cover: A Few Figs | From Thistles | Poems and Sonnets | By | Edna St. Vincent Millay. The foregoing is printed in black on a paper label within a triple-rule ornamental box, the first two lines in capitals, the rest in upper and lower case; the third

Bibliography

and fourth lines are in italic. Backbone: A Few Figs From Thistles—Millay. This is on a paper label, in capitals, reading lengthwise. Back cover blank. Top trimmed, other edges uncut. The book was printed at the Caxton Press.

Published December 15, 1922. Copies deposited December 30, 1922. There were two editions of this book. The first, described

A Few Figs From Thistles

POEMS AND SONNETS

By

Edna St. Vincent Millay

Poems and Sonnets

By

Edna St. Vincent Millay

NEW AND
ENLARGED EDITION

FRANK SHAY   STEWART KIDD
PUBLISHER   DISTRIBUTOR
NEW YORK   CINCINNATI

FRANK SHAY   STEWART KIDD
NEW YORK   CINCINNATI

CUT B   CUT C

See Collation No. 13 for explanation

above and title-page of which is shown as Cut B, was printed in a run of 2000 copies about December 8, 1922. The second, title-page of which is shown as Cut C, was printed in a run of 3000 copies about February 27, 1923. Excepting the change in title-page, and the omission of the numeral from the foot of p. 7 in the second, the two editions are identical. Shortly after the publication of the first edition, the limited edition (cf. Collation No. 14) was printed,

Edna St. Vincent Millay

and it was the title-page of the latter, but without the purple ink and without the border, that was used for the second edition.

Copies have appeared with the label on the backbone reading from top to bottom, and vice versa also. This is not a point of issue, as chance dictated the placing of the label. It was on the basis of this book, and *The Ballad of the Harp-Weaver*, and the eight sonnets that appeared in *American Poetry 1922 A Miscellany*, that Miss Millay was awarded the Pulitzer prize for 1922.

Contents: in addition to the nineteen poems of the 1921 edition (cf. Collation No. 7), this contains the following new poems, herein first printed in book form:

Recuerdo
MacDougal Street
Midnight Oil
To Kathleen

14. A FEW FIGS FROM THISTLES, Limited: 1922

A Few Figs From Thistles | Poems and Sonnets | By | Edna St. Vincent Millay | [*publisher's device*] | Frank Shay   Stewart Kidd | New York   Cincinnati

There is no date on the title-page. First line and device in purple. Last two lines in capitals, rest upper and lower case, the word "By" in italic. All within a double rule border.

Collation: Pp. 4 + 44, consisting of, after blue endsheet and two blank leaves not counted in pagination; p.[1] bastard title (limitation notice on verso); p.[3] title-page as above (copyright on verso); p.[5] half-title (acknowledgments on verso); p.[7] contents list (verso blank); pp. 9-34, text; p. 35, *Four Sonnets;* pp. 36-39, text of Four Sonnets; p.[40] publisher's device; pp.[41-44] blank; endsheet. Some copies have only one blank leaf at end.

8vo, size 6¼ x 9⅛. Binding of blue boards, white cloth back. Front cover: A Few Figs | From Thistles | Poems and Sonnets |

Bibliography

By | Edna St. Vincent Millay. The foregoing on a paper label, first two lines in capitals, rest upper and lower case, all within a double rule border. Backbone: A Few Figs From Thistles. This in capitals on a paper label affixed vertically. Back cover blank. Gilt top, other edges uncut. There is a border in purple around each page; the border on the title-page is in black. Printed at the Caxton Press on Deckle d'Aigle paper.

Published about December 16, 1922, after the regular trade edition (cf. Collation No. 13). The note on p. (2) indicates a printing of 250 copies. Except for the addition of the borders and limitation note, and the change in the title-page, the plates used here were those of the trade edition.

15. THE BALLAD OF THE HARP-WEAVER: 1922

The Ballad of The Harp-Weaver | By Edna St. Vincent Millay | New York: Printed for Frank Shay | and sold by him at Four Christopher St., | in the shadow of old Jefferson Market, 1922

Second and third words of third line, and first five words of fourth and fifth lines, in upper and lower case; remainder of fourth and fifth lines in large and small capitals; rest in capitals.

Collation; Pp. 20, consisting of, after endsheet; p.[1] bastard title (list of books on verso) ; p.[3] half-title (frontispiece on verso) ; p.[5] title-page as above (copyright on verso); pp.[7-16], text; pp.[17-20] blank; endsheet.

12mo, size $5\frac{1}{4}$ x $6\frac{3}{4}$. Binding of wrappers, extending over top and bottom edges $\frac{1}{2}$ inch and over fore edge $\frac{1}{16}$ inch. Front wrapper, in capitals: The Ballad of the Harp-Weaver | [*vignette of mother and child*] | By Edna St. Vincent Millay. Back wrapper blank. All edges trimmed.

[95]

Published December 29, 1922. Copies deposited December 30, 1922. Five hundred copies were run off with a slug reading *First Edition* at the foot of the verso of the title-page, and thereafter the slug was replaced by one reading *Second Edition* and fifteen hundred more copies were run off without other alteration.

Fifteen copies were bound in wrappers of each of the following colors: red, dark green, apple green, yellow, and blue, and all the other copies were bound in orange. It is almost certain that all seventy-five copies bound in colors other than orange were first edition copies, and that the entire second edition was bound in orange. Mr. Shay says so; I have never seen a second edition copy bound in any color but orange; and all the copies of the five other colors that I have seen were marked first edition. It is impossible to say which copies were bound first. No question of priority is involved in the color of the wrappers. Mr. Shay used them for window display purposes, as he did with the first edition of *A Few Figs From Thistles* (cf. Collation No. 5).

Japan Vellum Edition

Simultaneously with the first edition there were printed five copies on Japan vellum, having the same title-page as the regular edition, but differing from the regular edition in that the endsheets were omitted. These were signed on the half-title by the author. The only one I have seen was bound in red wrappers. Mr. Shay has no record or recollection of what other colors were used on these five copies.

16.   THE LAMP AND THE BELL,
Harpers: 1923

The Lamp | and The Bell | A Drama in Five Acts | By | Edna St. Vincent Millay | [*publishers' seal*] | Publishers | Harper & Brothers | New York and London

There is no date on the title-page. Word "Publishers" in upper and lower case italic; rest roman capitals.

Collation: Pp. 72, consisting of, after endsheet, p.[1] bastard title (list of books on verso) ; p.[3] title-page as above (copy-

Bibliography

right on verso) ; pp. 5-6, original cast; pp. 7-71, text; p.[72] blank; endsheet.

12mo, size 5¼ x 7¾. Bound in black cloth. Front cover lettered in gold capitals: THE LAMP | AND THE BELL | [acorn device] | EDNA ST. VINCENT MILLAY. Backbone lettered in gold capitals: THE | LAMP | AND | THE | BELL | [dash] | MILLAY | HARPERS. Back cover blank.

This first Harper & Brothers edition was composed of sheets bought from Mr. Frank Shay at the time he assigned his ownership of the copyright to Miss Millay in March 1923, with a cancel title-page printed by Harper & Brothers bearing the code letters G-X (July, 1923) on the verso thereof. There was only one edition during that month and bearing the code letters G-X. Thereafter the original Shay plates were used with changes of code letters, through several editions.

17. A FEW FIGS FROM THISTLES, Harpers: 1923

A Few Figs | From Thistles | Poems and Sonnets | By | Edna St. Vincent Millay | [publishers' seal] | Publishers | Harper & Brothers | New York and London | MCMXXIII
Sixth line is in upper and lower case italic; all rest in capitals.

Collation: Pp. 40 consisting of, after endsheet; pp.[1-2] blank; p.[3] title-page as above (copyright on verso) ; p.[5] acknowledgment note (verso blank) ; p.[7] contents list (verso blank) ; pp. 9-34, text; p. 35, *Four Sonnets;* pp. 36-39, text of Four Sonnets; p.[40] blank; endsheet.

8vo, size 5 x 7½. Bound in black ribbed cloth. Front cover lettered in gold capitals: A FEW FIGS | FROM THISTLES | [acorn device] | EDNA ST. VINCENT MILLAY. Backbone lettered in gold capitals: A | FEW | FIGS | FROM | THIS- | TLES [acorn device] |

Edna St. Vincent Millay

MILLAY | HARPERS. Back cover blank. Top and fore edges trimmed, lower edge untrimmed.

Printed, as the code letters G-X on the verso of the title-page indicate, in July of 1923, and published thereafter in due course. Frank Shay assigned his copyright of the 1922 edition to Miss Millay on March 31, 1923, and on July 10, 1923 John G. Kidd shipped the plates of the 1922 edition to Harpers. The text of this edition is therefore similar to the text of Collation No. 13.

18.   P O E M S : 1 9 2 3

Poems by | Edna St. Vincent Millay | [*device*] | London | Martin Secker | 1923

All the above in upper and lower case, the word "by" in italic.

Collation: Pp. 152, consisting of, after endsheet; pp.[1-2] blank; p.[3] bastard title (verso blank) ; p.[5] title-page as above (printer's notice on verso) ; pp. 7-10 *Contents*; p.[11] *Section One* (verso blank) ; pp. 13-47, text of Section One; p.[48] blank; p.[49] *Section Two* (verso blank) ; pp. 51-72, text of Section Two; p.[73] *Section Three* (verso blank) ; pp. 75-[146], text of Section Three; pp.[147-152] advertisements; endsheet.

12mo, size 4¾ x 7½. Bound in green cloth. Front and back covers blank except for two blind rules around edges. Backbone: [*two blind rules*] | POEMS | BY | EDNA | ST. VINCENT | MILLAY | [*device*] | SECKER | [*two blind rules*]. The foregoing in gold except as indicated, all in upper and lower case, the first two lines in italic. Top stained green. Fore edge trimmed, lower edge uncut.

Published in August, 1923. Second and subsequent editions carry a record of printing on the title-page. In 1927 this book was added to the Adelphi Library, published by Secker, as volume 29, and in that format has been reprinted several times. There is no American equivalent of this book, and the closest approach to it, *Poems Selected for Young People,* was not published until six years later.

The contents are of Miss Millay's own choosing, and it was at her special request that the enigmatic poem "Humoresque" was included. It is the only poem in the volume which had not previously appeared in book form. A summary of the contents follows:

Section One corresponds with *Renascence,* except that "Interim" and "The Suicide" have been omitted, and "Journey" has been added.

Section Two corresponds with the complete *A Few Figs From Thistles* (1922 edition) except that "Prisoner", "MacDougal Street", "Midnight Oil", and "To Kathleen" have been omitted, and "Humoresque" has been added.

Section Three corresponds with *Second April* except that "Rosemary" and "The Little Hill" have been omitted, and "Journey" has been transferred to Section One.

19. THE HARP-WEAVER AND OTHER POEMS: 1923

The Harp-Weaver | and | Other Poems | by | Edna St. Vincent Millay | [*publishers' seal*] | Publishers | Harper & Brothers | New York and London | MCMXXIII

All the above in capitals except sixth line, which is in upper and lower case italic.

Collation: Pp. x + 94, consisting of, after endsheet; p.[i] bastard title (list of books on verso) ; p.[iii] title-page as above (copyright on verso) ; p.[v] dedication (verso blank) ; pp. vii-x *Contents*; p.[1] *Part One* (verso blank) ; pp. 3-13, text of Part One; p.[14] blank; p.[15] *Part Two* (verso blank) ; pp. 17-35, text of Part Two; p.[36] blank; p.[37] *Part Three* (verso blank) ; pp. 39-49, text of Part Three; p.[50] blank; p.[51] *Part Four* (verso blank) ; pp. 53-74, text of Part Four; p.[75] *Part Five* (verso blank) ; pp. 77-93, text of Part Five; p.[94] blank; endsheet.

[99]

Edna St. Vincent Millay

12mo, size 5 x 7½. Bound in black cloth. Front cover lettered in gold capitals: THE HARP-WEAVER | AND | OTHER POEMS | [device] | EDNA ST. VINCENT MILLAY. Backbone lettered in gold capitals: THE | HARP- | WEAVER | AND | OTHER | POEMS | [device] | EDNA | ST. VINCENT | MILLAY. Back cover blank. Top and fore edges trimmed, lower edge uncut.

Published November 20, 1923. Copies deposited the same day. The first edition may be identified by the code letters K-X (November, 1923) on the verso of the title-page, and by the absence of the publishers' name from the foot of the backbone. The words "First Edition" are printed above the code letters, but are not to be relied upon solely. They were negligently retained through at least three subsequent printings indicated by different code letters, viz.: L-X (December, 1923); B-Y (February, 1924); K-Y (November, 1924). These later editions differ further from the first in that they carry the publishers' name at the foot of the backbone.

Contents, first book printing for all poems except those marked with an asterisk:

Part One
* My heart, being hungry
* Autumn chant
Nuit blanche
* Three songs from The Lamp and the Bell
The wood road
Feast
Souvenir
Scrub
The Goosegirl
The Dragonfly

Part Two
* Departure
The Return from Town
A Visit to the Asylum
The Spring and the Fall
The Curse
Keen
* The Betrothal

Bibliography

She filled her arms with wood, and set her chin
The white bark writhed and sputtered like a fish
The wagon stopped before the house; she heard
Then cautiously she pushed the cellar door
One way there was of muting in the mind
She let them leave their jellies at the door
Not over-kind nor over-quick in study
She had forgotten how the August night
It came into her mind, seeing how the snow
Tenderly, in those times, as though she fed
From the wan dream, that was her waking day,
She had a horror he would die at night
There was upon the sill a pencil mark
The doctor asked her what she wanted done
Gazing upon him now, severe and dead,

20.   ARIA DA CAPO, Appleton: 1924

Aria da Capo | A Play in One Act | By | Edna St. Vincent Millay | [*publishers' seal*] | D. Appleton and Company | New York [*two devices*] MCMXXIV
All the above in capitals, except second and third lines which are upper and lower case italic.

Collation: Pp. 48, consisting of; p.[1] bastard title (list of little theatre plays on verso) ; p.[3] title-page as above (copyright on verso) ; p.[5] *Persons (Original Cast* on verso) ; pp. 7-35, text; p.[36] blank; pp. 37-38, *Author's Note;* pp. 39-48, suggestions for production.

12mo, size 5⅛ x 7½. Binding of heavy white art paper wrappers, with five vertical stripes on left side of front, and lettering on right side, in orange. Front cover: Aria da Capo | By | Edna St. Vincent | Millay | [*publishers' seal*] | The Appleton | Little Theatre Plays | No. 9 | Edited by | Grace Adams. The foregoing in roman capitals, except second and eighth lines which are upper and lower case italic. The seal is also printed in orange on the back wrapper. Advertisements on verso of front and recto of back wrappers. All edges trimmed.

Bibliography

Published in February, 1924. The first Appleton edition may be identified by a numeral (1) following the last line of the text on p. 48. The copyright year is 1920, carried over from the copyright of the unpublished play. This edition is not a first printing for any part of the contents.

21. ARIA DA CAPO, Harpers: 1924

Aria da Capo | A Play in One Act | By | Edna St. Vincent Millay | [*publishers' seal*] | Publishers | Harper & Brothers | New York and London

There is no date on the title-page. Word "Publishers" upper and lower case italic; all rest roman capitals.

Collation: Pp. VIII + 56, consisting of, after endsheet, pp. [I-II] blank; p.[III] bastard title (list of books on verso) ; p.[v] title-page as above (copyright on verso) ; p.[VII] half-title (verso: *Persons*) ; pp. 1-51, text; pp.[52-56] blank; endsheet.

8vo, size 5¼ x 7⅝. Bound in black ribbed cloth. Front cover lettered in gold capitals: ARIA DA CAPO | [*device*] | EDNA ST. VINCENT MILLAY. Backbone lettered in gold capitals: ARIA | DA | CAPO | EDNA | ST. V. | MILLAY | HARPER (sic) . Back cover blank. All edges trimmed.

Printed, as the code letters B-Y on the verso of the title-page indicate, in February, 1924, and issued shortly thereafter. This edition contains the Author's Note on pp. 37-38, and Suggestions for the Production of "Aria da Capo" on pp. 39-51. This is the first edition of *Aria da Capo* published by Harper & Brothers.

22. RENASCENCE, Goudy: 1924

Renascence | A Poem by | Edna St. Vincent Millay | Printed for the First Time in | Separate Form by Frederick | & Bertha Goudy on the | Handpress on which |

Edna St. Vincent Millay

William Morris | Printed the | Kelmscott | Chaucer | [*printer's ornament*] | At the Anderson Galleries | New York: March MCMXXIV

Title-page in capitals throughout.

Collation; Pp. 12, consisting of, after blank leaf not counted in pagination; p.[1] title-page as above (verso: *Copyright 1912 by Mitchell Kennerley*); p.[3] bibliographical note (verso blank); pp. 5-[11], text; p.[12] colophon; blank leaf.

8vo, size 4 x 9. Binding of blue paper wrappers, without printing, sewed with heavy silk. Top trimmed, other edges uncut. Text in Garamont Italic, bibliographical note in Kennerley type, on Hand Made British paper.

The colophon reads as follows: This copy is printed by Frederick & Bertha Goudy on the Handpress Formerly Owned By William Morris on which the Kelmscott Chaucer was printed—during an Exhibition of the Press at the Anderson Galleries, New York, March 1924. Copies will be printed and sold only during the Exhibition at the close of which the type will be distributed. This copy is No. (here follows number in ink).

According to Mr. Goudy, "maybe 180 or 185 in all" were printed. None were signed by Miss Millay at the exhibition; Mr. Goudy signed merely his initials beneath the number of each copy. If precedence is of any moment in this first separate appearance, it must be given in numerical order, because copies were run off at intervals through a few weeks' period.

23. THE HARP-WEAVER, English:
1924

The Harp-Weaver by | Edna St. Vincent Millay | [*printer's device*] | London | Martin Secker | 1924

Bibliography

All the above in upper and lower case; the word "by" in italic.

Collation: Pp. 104 consisting of, after endsheet; pp.[1-2] blank; p.[3] bastard title (verso: *Uniform with this | Poems*) ; p.[5] title-page as above (printer's notice on verso) ; pp. 7-10, *Contents;* p.[11] *Part One* (verso blank) ; pp. 13-23, text of Part One; p.[24] blank; p.[25] *Part Two* (verso blank) ; pp. 27-44, text of Part Two; p.[45] *Part Three* (verso blank) ; pp. 47-56, text of Part Three; p.[57] *Part Four* (verso blank) ; pp. 59-80, text of Part Four; p.[81] *Part Five* (verso blank) ; pp. 83-99, text of Part Five; p.[100] printer's imprint; pp.[101-104] advertisements; endsheet.

12mo, size $4\frac{7}{8}$ x $7\frac{1}{2}$. Bound in green cloth, with two blind-stamped rules around front and back covers. Backbone: [*two blind-stamped rules*] | THE | HARP- | WEAVER | BY | EDNA | ST. VINCENT | MILLAY | [*ornament*] | SECKER | [*two blind-stamped rules*]. The foregoing in upper and lower case, first four lines in italic, all type in gold. Top stained green. Fore edge trimmed, lower edge uncut.

Published in March, 1924. There was only one printing, in all copies of which the word "before" was omitted from the first line on p. 87. In all other respects this English edition contains the same text as the American edition of *The Harp-Weaver and other Poems.*

24. THE LAMP AND THE BELL, Appleton:1924

The Lamp | and the Bell | A Drama in Five Acts | By | Edna St. Vincent Millay | [*publishers' seal*] | D. Appleton and Company | New York :: :: MCMXXIV

All the above in capitals, except third and fourth lines which are upper and lower case italic.

Collation: Pp. 80, consisting of; p.[1] bastard title (verso

blank); p.[3] title-page as above (verso: *Copyright 1921*);
pp.[5-6] *Characters*; pp. 7-79, text; p.[80] advertisement.

8vo, size 4¾ x 7¼. Binding of heavy white art paper wrappers,
with five vertical bars on left side of front, and lettering on
right, in dark green: The Lamp | and the Bell | By | Edna
St. Vincent | Millay | [*publishers' seal*] | The Appleton | Little
Theater Plays | No. 10 | Edited by | Grace Adams. Third and
ninth lines in upper and lower case italic, rest in roman capitals. Advertisements on verso of front cover and recto of back
cover; back wrapper bears seal in green. All edges trimmed.

Published in spring of 1924. The first Appleton edition may be
identified by a numeral (1) following the last line of text on p. 79.

25.   DISTRESSING DIALOGUES:
1924

Distressing | Dialogues | by | Nancy Boyd | With a Preface
by | Edna St. Vincent Millay | [*publishers' seal*] | Pub-
lishers | Harper & Brothers | New York and London
There is no date on the title-page. The fifth and seventh
lines are in italic upper and lower case; rest in roman capitals.

Collation: Pp. viii + 294, consisting of, after endsheet, one
blank leaf not counted in pagination; p.[I] bastard title (verso
blank); p.[III] title-page as above (copyright on verso); pp.
v-vi, *Contents;* p.[vII] *Preface* (verso blank); p.[1] story title
(verso blank); pp. 3-290, text; pp.[291-2] advertisements; pp.
[293-4] blank; endsheet. Included in the pagination of the text
are 22 unnumbered leaves carrying story titles on rectos, the
versos being blank. Pp.[12], [26], [38], [54], [82], [94], [134],
[160], [184], and [254] are also blank.

12mo, size 5 x 7½. Bound in black cloth, lettered in gold
capitals on front cover: DISTRESSING | DIALOGUES | [*device*] |
NANCY BOYD. Backbone lettered in gold capitals: DISTRESSING |

Bibliography

DIALOGUES | [*device*] | NANCY BOYD | [*rule*] | HARPERS | [*rule*].
Back cover blank. All edges trimmed.

Published September 22, 1924. Copies deposited September 23, 1924. The first edition may be identified by the words "First Edition" and the code letters G-Y (July, 1924) on the verso of the title-page.

The brief preface is signed "Edna St. Vincent Millay. Tokyo, May 6, 1924." Its endorsement of the book is partially explained by the intelligence that Nancy Boyd is a pseudonym of Miss Millay.

Contents (with date of appearance in *Vanity Fair*) :

I Like Americans	August, 1922
Honor Bright	December, 1922
Our All-American Almanac and Prophetic Messenger	March, 1923
The Implacable Aphrodite	March, 1921
The Same Boat	June, 1921
No Bigger than a Man's Hand	September, 1922
The Greek Dance	August, 1921
Art and How to Fake It	October, 1921
Powder, Rouge and Lipstick	September, 1921
Out of Reach of the Baby	April, 1922
Look Me Up	October, 1922
For Winter, for Summer	December, 1921
"Madame a Tort!"	February, 1923
"Two Souls with but a Single Thought"	January, 1923
Knock Wood	June, 1922
Tea for the Muse	January, 1922
Rolls and Salt	January, 1921
How to Be Happy Though Good	May, 1922
Here Comes the Bride	February, 1922
Breakfast in Bed	May, 1921
Ships and Sealing Wax	March, 1922
Cordially Yours	November, 1921

26. RENASCENCE, Harpers: 1925

Renascence | and | Other Poems | by | Edna St. Vincent Millay | [*publishers' seal*] | Publishers | Harper & Brothers | New York and London

Edna St. Vincent Millay

There is no date on the title-page, which is in capitals throughout.

Collation: Pp. VI + 74, consisting of, after endsheet; p.[I] bastard title (list of books on verso) ; p.[III] title-page as above (copyright on verso) ; p.[V] contents list (verso blank) ; pp. 1-73, text; p.[74] blank; endsheet.

8vo, size 5 1/16 x 7 7/16. Bound in black cloth. Front cover lettered in gold capitals: RENASCENCE | [*device*] | EDNA ST. VINCENT MILLAY. Backbone lettered in gold capitals: RENASCENCE | [*device*] | MILLAY | HARPERS. Back cover blank. Top and fore edges trimmed, lower edge rough trimmed.

Printed, as the code letters A-Z on the verso of the title-page indicate, in January of 1925, and published March 25, 1925. The plates of the original Kennerley edition were used in this first edition published by Harper & Brothers; the text is therefore similar to the text of Collation No. 3.

27. SECOND APRIL, Harpers: 1925

Second April | Edna St. Vincent Millay | [*publishers' seal*] | Publishers | Harper & Brothers | New York and London

There is no date on the title-page, which is in capitals throughout.

Collation: Pp. X + 114, consisting of; pp.[I-II] blank; p.[III] bastard title (list of books on verso) ; p.[V] title-page as above (copyright on verso) ; p.[VII] dedication (verso blank) ; p.[IX] contents list (verso blank) ; pp.[1]-112, text; pp.[113-114] blank.

8vo, size 5 1/16 x 7 7/16. Bound in black cloth. Front cover lettered in gold capitals: SECOND APRIL | [*device*] | EDNA ST. VINCENT MILLAY. Backbone lettered in gold capitals: SECOND | APRIL | [*device*] | MILLAY | HARPERS. Back cover blank. Top and fore edges trimmed, lower edge rough trimmed.

Bibliography

Printed, as the code letters A-Z on the verso of the title-page indicate, in January of 1925, and published March 25, 1925. The plates of the original Kennerley edition were used in this first edition published by Harper & Brothers; the text is therefore similar to the text of Collation No. 9.

28. THREE PLAYS: 1926

Three Plays | By | Edna St. Vincent Millay | [*publishers'
seal*] | Harper & Brothers Publishers | New York and
London | MCMXXVI

Title-page in capitals throughout. First line, and seal, in red.

Collation: Pp. x + 150, consisting of, after endsheet; pp.
[I-II] blank; p.[III] bastard title (list of books on verso) ; p.[V]
blank; p.[VI] frontispiece; p.[VII] title-page as above (copyright
on verso) ; p.[IX] *Contents* (verso blank) ; p.[1] play title (*Persons* on verso) ; pp. 3-14, text of Two Slatterns and a King;
p.[15] play title (*Persons* on verso) ; pp. 17-44, text of Aria da
Capo; p.[45] play title (verso blank) ; pp. 47-8, dramatis personae; pp. 49-147, text of The Lamp and the Bell; pp.[148-150]
blank; endsheet.

16mo, size 5 x 7½. Binding of batik paper over boards, black
cloth back and corners. Covers blank. Backbone: [*three rules*] |
Three | Plays | [*device*] | Edna | St. Vincent | Millay | [*rule*] |
Harpers | [*three rules*]. The foregoing on a paper label, first
two lines in capitals, rest upper and lower case, with last
line in italic. Top stained red. Fore and lower edges rough
trimmed. Also bound in blue limp leather, front cover blind-
stamp ruled into six panels, with gold figure of harp player
in center. Backbone lettered in gold capitals: [*blind rule*] |
THREE | PLAYS | [*gold rule*] | EDNA | ST. VINCENT | MILLAY |
[*blind rule*] | [*gold ornament*] | HARPERS | [*blind rule*]. Back
cover blank. Top edge gilt. Fore and lower edges rough
trimmed. Different bindings issued simultaneously.

Edna St. Vincent Millay

Published October 20, 1926. Copies deposited October 12, 1926. The first edition may be identified by the words "First Edition" and the code letters I-A (September, 1926) on the verso of the title-page. First collected edition of the three plays.

29.   THE KING'S HENCHMAN, Score: 1926

The | King's Henchman | Lyric Drama in Three Acts | Book by | Edna St. Vincent Millay | Music by | Deems Taylor | Opus 19 | [*publishers' device, with words* "Fischer edition"] | No. 5725 | J. Fischer & Bro., New York | 119 West 40th Street | 3, New Street, Birmingham, England. Printed in U.S.A.

There is no date on the title-page. First three lines, and words "Opus 19" and "No." in upper and lower case; all rest in capitals.

Collation: Pp. x + 280, consisting of pp.[I-II] blank; p.[III] title-page as above (verso: *Copyright 1926 by J. Fischer & Bro.*) ; p.[V] *Cast of Characters* (verso blank) ; p.[VII] *Index of Scenes* (verso blank) ; p.[IX] dedication (verso blank) ; pp. 1-279, text; p.[280] blank.

4to, size 7½ x 10¾. Binding of stiff gray wrappers, black cloth back, with design, picturing a knight and lady on a charger, on front cover in black and four colors. Lettering in black: Deems Taylor | The King's | Henchman | Lyric Drama in Thr [*design covers last two letters*] Acts | Book By | Edna St. Vincent Millay | J. Fischer | & Bro. | New York. The last three lines are in the lower left corner. The cover was printed from a hand-executed painting.

Published December 31, 1926. Copies deposited January 6, 1927. The foregoing is a description of the first edition, which contains the complete score and the full text. After the presentation of the opera

Bibliography

at the Metropolitan on February 17, 1927 there was a second printing, in March, 1927, carrying a record of the printing on the verso
of the title-page. The second printing is of interest because it includes a list of the cast of the first performance, which did not
appear in the first edition. Some minor changes were made in the
score, and the collation differs from that of the first edition. Collation: Pp. x + 276, consisting of pp.[I-II] blank; p.[III] title-page as
above (copyright on verso); p.[V] *Cast of Characters*; pp.[VI-VII] *The
Cast*; p.[VIII] *Index of Scenes*; p.[IX] dedication (verso blank); pp.
1-274, text; pp.[275-276] blank.

It must be noted that the *Cast of Characters* here means *dramatis
personae*, and *The Cast*—pp.[VI-VII]—is a list of the names of the
performers. In respect to size, binding, and paper the two printings
are similar.

30.   THE KING'S HENCHMAN,
Libretto: 1927

The | King's Henchman | Lyric Drama | In Three Acts |
Book by | Edna St. Vincent Millay | Music by | Deems
Taylor | [*publishers' seal, with words "Fischer Edition"*]
| No. 5901 | Libretto .35 | Piano-Vocal Score 5.00 | (Copy-
right, 1926, by J. Fischer & Bro.) | Published by | J.
Fischer & Bro.—119 West 40th Street, - N. Y. | 3, New
Street, Birmingham, England | Copyright, 1927, by Edna
St. Vincent Millay | British (International) Copyright
Secured.

*First eight lines, and publishers' name in fourteenth line,
in capitals; rest upper and lower case, the thirteenth line in
italic, and the last line rubber stamped.*

Collation: Pp. 32, consisting of, p.[1], title-page as above;
pp. 2-3, *Synopsis*; p. 4, *Cast of Characters*; pp. 5-31, text; p.[32],
blank.

8vo, size 6⅝ x 10½. Binding of blue wrappers. Front cover:

Edna St. Vincent Millay

Libretto of | the | King's Henchman | Lyric Drama | in three acts | book by | Edna St. Vincent Millay | Music by | Deems Taylor | (illustration) | Published by | J. Fischer & Bro.—119 West 40th Street,—N. Y. | 3, New Street, Birmingham, England. The words "Libretto" and "J. Fischer & Bro." in capitals, rest upper and lower case, with fourth, fifth, and tenth lines in italic. The illustration is a reduced cut of the colored illustration that appears on the cover of the score (cf. Collation No. 29). Back cover bears advertisement of Harper & Brothers. The verso of the front cover and recto of the back cover are blank. All edges trimmed.

Published February 10, 1927. There are no copies in the Library of Congress. The publishers say that there were three printings of this libretto, but they have no record of changes, and I have not been able to discover any. Like the Rullman libretto following, this libretto does not contain the lyrics of the complete play.

30A.   RULLMAN LIBRETTO

The | King's Henchman | Lyric Drama | in three acts | book by | Edna St. Vincent Millay | music by | Deems Taylor | Copyright 1926, 1927 by Edna St Vincent Millay | Published by | Fred. Rullman, Inc., New York, N. Y.

There is no publication date on the title-page. All except ninth line, which is in upper and lower case, in capitals.

Collation: Pp. 32, consisting of; p.[1] title-page as above; pp. 2-30, text; p.[31] Harpers advertisement; p. [32] blank.

8vo, size 8¼ x 11¼. Issued in gray-green wrappers with Rullman standard libretto pictorial design, carrying type insert of title in right center.

Two states of this libretto, displaying several minor variations, have come to light. One, collated above, carries a double copyright date, (i.e. 1926, 1927) on the title-page; the other carries only the date 1927. No exact information is available, but on the basis of internal evidence, it is highly probable that the issue collated here is the earlier. First put on sale at the premier performance of the opera at the Metropolitan on February 17, 1927. Subsequent, therefore, to foregoing Fischer libretto, but with same incomplete text.

31.   THE KING'S HENCHMAN: 1927

The King's | Henchman | A Play in Three Acts | by Edna St. Vincent Millay | [*publishers' seal*] | Harper & Brothers Publishers | New York and London | MCMXXVII

The first letter is a two line capital; the second line begins to the right of the stem of the capital "T". The first two lines and the seal are in red. The first four lines are modified black letter upper and lower case, rest in capitals.

Collation: Pp. x + 134, consisting of, after white endsheet; pp.[I-II] blank; p.[III] bastard title (list of books on verso); p.[V] blank; p.[VI] frontispiece; p.[VII] title-page as above (copyright on verso); p.[ix] dedication (verso blank); p.[1] half-title, with *Time* and *Place* (*Persons* on verso); pp. 3-[132], text; pp.[133-134] blank; endsheet.

12mo, size 5⅛ x 7½. Binding of blue-gray boards, black cloth back and corners. Covers blank. Backbone, on paper label, upper and lower cast except last line: [*rule*] | the | King's | Hench- | man | by | Edna | St. Vincent | Millay | [*rule*] | Harpers. Top stained orange-yellow, fore and lower edges rough-trimmed.

Published February 16, 1927. Copies deposited February 18, 1927. The first edition may be identified by the words "First Edition" and the code letters B-B, (February, 1927) on the verso of the title-page. There were two other printings in the same month, both of which bear the letters B-B but do not have the words "First Edition." This collation describes the first complete edition of the play, without the music.

32.   THE KING'S HENCHMAN,
Limited: 1927

Title-page identical with that of the trade edition.

Collation: Pp. VIII + 134, consisting of, after buff end-sheet; p.[I] bastard title (list of books on verso) ; p.[III] blank; p.[IV] frontispiece; p.[V] title-pageasabove (copyrighton verso) ; p.[VII] dedication (verso blank) ; p.[I] half-title, with *Time* and *Place* (*Persons* on verso) ; pp. 3-[132], text; pp.[133-134] blank; endsheet.

8vo, size 6½ x 10¼. Binding of figured red boards, black cloth back. Covers blank. Backbone: [*fancy rule*] | The | King's | Hench- | man | by | Edna | St. Vincent | Millay | [*fancy rule*] | Autographed | Limited | Edition | No. [*here follows number in red ink*]. The foregoing on a paper label, with rules in orange, and first eight lines in modified black letter. All edges untrimmed.

Tipped in between p.[II] and p.[III] is a limitation leaf recto of which reads: This edition of The King's Henchman printed from newly set Caslon type is limited to one hundred and fifty-eight copies on Tuscany hand-made paper, of which one hundred and fifty copies are for sale and eight for private distribution. Each volume is numbered and has been signed by the author. This volume is number (here follows number and signature in ink) .

This limited edition was published one day later than the trade edition, to wit, on February 17, 1927. The text is identical with that of the trade edition.

JAPAN VELLUM EDITION

Title-page identical with that of the trade edition.
Collation: Pp. x + 134, consisting of, after gray-green end-

Bibliography

sheet; pp.[i-ii] blank; p.[iii] bastard title (list of books on verso) ; p.[v] blank; p.[vi] frontispiece; p.[vii] title-page as above (copyright on verso) ; p.[ix] dedication (verso blank) ; p.[1] half-title, with *Time* and *Place* (*Persons* on verso) ; pp. 3-[132], text; pp.[133-134] blank; endsheet. Tipped in between p.[iv] and p.[v] is a limitation leaf.

4to, size 6⅜ x 9¾. Binding of figured gray boards, white linen back. Covers blank. Backbone bears a paper label similar to that of the preceding limited edition. All edges uncut.

Published February 17, 1927. The recto of the limitation leaf reads: This edition of The King's Henchman printed from newly set Caslon type is limited to thirty-one copies on Shizuoka Imperial Japan vellum of which twenty-six copies lettered from A to Z are for sale and the remaining five unlettered copies are for private distribution. Each copy of this edition is signed by the author and contains in addition a signed artist's proof on Japanese tissue of an original woodcut by Harry Cimino. This is copy letter (here follows letter and signature in ink). Verso of limitation leaf blank. The proof of a woodcut referred to is the frontispiece.

33. THE KING'S HENCHMAN,
Artists': 1927

Title-page identical with that of the trade edition.

Collation: Pp. xii + 132, consisting of, after dark gray-green endsheet; p.[i] bastard title (list of books on verso) ; p.[iii] bibliographical note (verso blank) ; p.[v] blank; p.[vi] frontispiece; p.[vii] title-page as above (copyright on verso) ; p.[ix] dedication (verso blank) ; p.[xi] facsimile of program (verso blank) ; p.[1] half-title, with *Time* and *Place* (*Persons* on verso) ; pp. 3-[132], text; endsheet. Tipped in between p.[iv] and p.[v] is a limitation leaf printed on the recto; verso blank. A facsimile page of score manuscript, folded twice to page size, is tipped in between p.[xii] and p.[1]. Three etchings, each tipped in and protected by a tissue guard, face pp. 3, 39, and 81 respectively.

12mo, size 6⅜ x 10. Binding of light gray-green boards, buckram back and corners. Covers blank. Backbone: [*fancy rule*] | The | King's | Hench- | man | by | Edna | St. Vincent | Millay | [*fancy rule*] | Artists' | Edition | No. [*here follows number in red ink*]. The foregoing on a paper label, last two lines italic capitals, rest upper and lower case. All edges uncut.

Printed, as the code letters C-B on the verso of the title-page indicate, in March, 1927, and issued shortly thereafter. The limitation leaf reads: This Artists' Edition of The King's Henchman printed from type on Tuscany hand-made paper is limited to five hundred numbered copies autographed by the author. This volume is number (here follows number and signature in ink). The bibliographical note on p.[III] expands the foregoing statement by stating that each copy contains a facsimile page from the operatic score signed by the composer, Deems Taylor, and three proof etchings of Joseph Urban's stage sets for the three acts of the opera.

34. THE KING'S HENCHMAN, English: 1927

The King's Henchman | A Play in Three Acts by | Edna St. Vincent Millay | [*publisher's seal*] | Jonathan Cape | Thirty Bedford Square, London

There is no date on the title-page. All the above in upper and lower case, the word "by" in italic.

Collation: Pp. 96 consisting of, after endsheet; p.[1] bastard title (list of books on verso) ; p.[3] title-page as above (verso: *First published in MCMXXVII* and printer's notice) ; p.[5] dedication (verso blank) ; p.[7] half-title, with *Time* and *Place* (*Persons* on verso) ; pp. 9-96, text; endsheet.

12mo, size 5 x 7⁹⁄₁₆. Bound in orange cloth. Front cover blank. Backbone, in blue, lettered from top to bottom, in capitals: THE KING'S HENCHMAN | EDNA ST. VINCENT MILLAY. At foot of backstrip: JONATHAN | CAPE. Publisher's seal in blind on back cover. Top stained orange. All edges trimmed.

Published in spring of 1927. This English edition contains the same text as the American edition.

35. FEAR: 1927

Reflections on the Sacco-Vanzetti Tragedy | [*three rules*] | Fear | By Edna St. Vincent Millay | [*rule*] | Vanzetti's Last Statement | By William G. Thompson | [*rule*] | Psychology and Justice | By John Dewey | [*rule*] | The Martyrs of Massachusetts | By C. I. Claflin | [*three rules*] | Published by | The Sacco-Vanzetti Defense Committee | P.O. Box 93, Hanover St. Station, Boston, Mass.

The front wrapper serves as title-page, and carries no date. All the above is set within a triple rule border. The authors' names, and the second, ninth, and tenth lines are in capitals; rest upper and lower case.

Collation: Pp. 16, consisting of p.[1] title-page as above (verso blank); pp.[3]-15, text; p.[16] blank.

8vo, size 6⅛ x 9⅛, wire stitched. *Fear* occupies pp.[3]-6, both inclusive. It is the same article that appeared in the magazine *Outlook,* for November 9, 1927. I have been unable to ascertain the exact date of publication, but I can say that this pamphlet was issued after the original magazine appearance, and before the end of the year 1927.

SEPARATE EDITION

Fear | by | Edna St. Vincent Millay | [*printer's device*] | Distributed by | Sacco-Vanzetti National League | 104 Fifth Avenue | New York City

There is no date on the title-page. All the above is set

Edna St. Vincent Millay

within a double rule border. Second and fourth lines in italic upper and lower case; rest in roman capitals.

Collation: Pp. 4, consisting of p.[1] title-page as above; pp.[2-4], text.

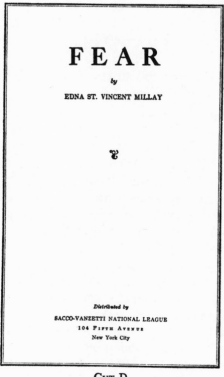

CUT D
See Collation No. 35

Folio, size 6 x 9. This leaflet contains the same text as the Millay contribution to the foregoing item. It was issued subsequent to the latter, probably late in 1927. It is the only separate printing of a prose article by Miss Millay. See Cut D.

Bibliography

36. THE BUCK IN THE SNOW: 1928

The | Buck in the Snow | & Other Poems by | Edna St. Vincent Millay | [*publishers' seal*] | Harper & Brothers Publishers | New York and London | MCMXXVIII

First, second, and third lines, and seal, in red. First and third lines and words "Publishers" and "and" in italic upper and lower case; places in roman upper and lower case, rest in capitals.

Collation: Pp. VI + 72, consisting of, after endsheet and one blank leaf not counted in pagination; p.[I] bastard title (list of books on verso); p.[III] title-page as above (copyright on verso); pp. V-VI, *Contents;* p.[1] *Part One* (verso blank); pp. 3-28, text of Part One; p.[29] *Part Two* (verso blank); pp. 31-36, text of Part Two; p.[37] *Part Three* (verso blank); pp. 39-59, text of Part Three; p.[60] blank; p.[61] *Part Four* (verso blank); pp. 63-69, text of Part Four; p.[70] trade mark; pp.[71-72] blank; endsheet.

8vo, size 5 x 7½. Binding of blue-gray boards, black cloth back and corners. Covers blank. Backbone: [*three rules*] | The | Buck | in the | Snow | And Other | Poems | [*ornament*] | Edna | St. Vincent | Millay | [*rule*] | Harpers | [*three rules*]. The foregoing on a white paper label, first three lines in capitals, rest upper and lower case. Top stained orange, fore and lower edges trimmed. Also bound in blue limp leather, front cover blind-stamp ruled into six panels, with gold figure of harp player in center. Backbone lettered in gold capitals: [*blind rule*] | THE | BUCK | IN THE | SNOW | [*gold rule*] | EDNA ST. VINCENT | MILLAY | [*blind rule*] | [*gold ornament*] | HARPERS | [*blind rule*]. Back cover blank. Top edge gilt. Fore and lower edges rough trimmed. Different bindings issued simultaneously.

Published September 27, 1928. Copies deposited September 28,

Edna St. Vincent Millay

1928. The first edition may be identified by the words "First Edition" and the code letters I-C (September, 1928), on the verso of the title-page.

Contents, first book printing for all poems except those marked with asterisk:

Part One

Moriturus
Song
To the wife of a sick friend
The Bobolink
The Hawkweed
To a friend estranged from me
The road to Avrillé
For Pao-Chin
Northern April
There at dusk I found you
Being young and green
Mist in the valley
The hardy garden
The Pigeons
The Buck in the Snow

Part Two

The Anguish
* Justice denied in Massachusetts
Hangman's Oak
Wine from these grapes
To those without pity

Part Three

Dawn
To a young girl
Evening on Lesbos
Dirge without music
Memory of Cassis
Portrait
Winter night
The Cameo
Counting-out rhyme
The Plum Gatherer
West County Song

Bibliography

Pueblo Pot
When Cæsar fell
Lethe
On first having heard the skylark
To a musician

Part Four

Sonnet—Life, were thy pains as are the pains of hell
* Sonnet—Grow not too high, grow not too far from home
* Sonnet to Gath—Country of hunchbacks!—where the strong straight
  spine
* The Pioneer—Upon this marble bust that is not I
  To Jesus on his birthday—For this your mother sweated in the cold
* Sonnet—Not that it matters, not that my heart's cry
  On hearing a symphony of Beethoven—Sweet sounds, oh beautiful
  music, do not cease!

37. THE BUCK IN THE SNOW,
Limited: 1928

Title-page identical with that of the trade edition.

Collation: Pp. VIII + 72, consisting of, after gray-green endsheet; p.[I] bastard title (verso blank); p.[III] bibliographical
note (list of books on verso); p.[V] title-page (copyright on
verso); pp. [VII-VIII] *Contents;* p.[1] *Part One;* through remainder of book the collation is identical with that of the
trade edition. Tipped in between p.[II] and p.[III] is a leaf
of Japan vellum on recto of which are the number of the
copy and the signature of the author, in ink; verso blank.

8vo, size 6 x 9. Binding of light gray-green boards, linen
back. Covers blank. Backbone: [*wavy rule*] | The | Buck | in
the | Snow | [*device*] | Millay | [*dotted rule*] | Harpers | [*wavy
rule*]. The foregoing on paper label, in capitals. Top edge uncut, other edges trimmed.

Both this and the ultra-limited edition following were published
simultaneously with the trade edition, and bear the words "First

Edition" and the code letters I-C on the verso of the title-page. The bibliographical note on p.[III] reads: This first edition of The Buck in the Snow set up and printed from type, consists of five hundred and fifteen copies, each numbered and signed by the author. Thirty-six copies are printed on Japan vellum, of which only the first thirty-one copies are for sale; four hundred and seventy-nine copies are printed on Arches hand-made paper, of which only numbers thirty-seven to five hundred and five are for sale. The type has been destroyed.

JAPAN VELLUM EDITION

The ultra-limited edition of 36 copies is the same as the foregoing, with the obvious distinction in the stock on which it is printed. The binding is of boards, with parchment back and leather label.

38.   THE BUCK IN THE SNOW,
English: 1928

Edna St. Vincent Millay | The | Buck in the Snow | and other poems | London | Harper & Brothers | 35 Great Russell Street | 1928
Fifth and seventh lines in upper and lower case, rest in capitals. Third line in large open face.

Collation: Pp. vi + 72, consisting of, after endsheet and one blank leaf not counted in pagination; p.[I] bastard title (list of books on verso) ; p.[III] title-page as above (printer's notice on verso) ; pp. v-vi, *Contents;* p.[1] *Part One* (verso blank) ; pp. 3-28, text of Part One; p.[29] *Part Two* (verso blank) ; pp. 31-36, text of Part Two; p.[37] *Part Three* (verso blank) ; pp. 39-59, text of Part Three; p.[60] blank; p.[61] *Part Four* (verso blank) ; pp. 63-69, text of Part Four; p.[70-72] blank; endsheet.

8vo, size 5 x 7½. Bound in light blue cloth. Covers blank. Backbone lettered in gold capitals: THE | BUCK | IN THE | SNOW

Bibliography

| [*device*] | EDNA | ST. VINCENT | MILLAY | HARPERS. Top stained yellow. Fore and lower edges untrimmed.

Published in November, 1928. This English edition contains the same text as the American edition.

39.   P O E M S   S E L E C T E D   F O R
             Y O U N G   P E O P L E :   1 9 2 9

Edna St. Vincent Millay's | Poems | Selected for Young People | Illustrations and Decorations by | J. Paget-Fredericks | [*vignette*] | Harper & Brothers Publishers | New York and London | 1929
Second and fourth lines in capitals; all the rest in upper and lower case, the third line and the word "and" in the seventh line in italics.

Collation: Pp. x + 118, consisting of, after decorated endsheet; p.[I] bastard title (verso blank); p.[III] title-page as above (copyright on verso); pp.[v-vI] illustrations; pp. VII-IX, *Contents;* p.[x] blank; p.[1] *Part One* (illustration on verso); pp. 3-34, text of Part One; p.[35] *Part Two* (verso blank); pp. 37-59, text of Part Two; p.[60] blank; p.[61] *Part Three* (verso blank); pp. 63-69, text of Part Three; p.[70] blank; p.[71] *Part Four* (verso blank); pp. 73-88, text of Part Four; p.[89] *Part Five* (verso: *Memorial to D. C.*); pp. 91-97, text of Part Five; p.[98] blank; p.[99] *Part Six* (verso blank); pp. 101-113, text of Part Six; pp.[114-118] blank; decorated endsheet. Tipped in between p.[II] and p.[III] is a leaf of glazed paper with a colored illustration on the verso; the recto is blank. Pp. 30 and [54] are full page illustrations.

8vo, size 5¾ x 8¾. Bound in bright orange cloth. Front cover: EDNA ST. VINCENT MILLAY'S | —POEMS— | SELECTED FOR YOUNG PEOPLE | [*vignette*]. The foregoing in black, lettering in upper and lower case roman, roman capitals, and upper and lower

Edna St. Vincent Millay

case italic respectively. Backbone: EDNA | ST. VINCENT | MILLAY'S | POEMS | SELECTED | FOR | YOUNG | PEOPLE | [*device*] | [*rule*] | HARPERS. The foregoing in black, fourth and ninth lines in roman capitals, rest upper and lower case, the fifth to eighth lines in italic. Back cover blank. Top trimmed, fore and lower edges rough trimmed.

Published November 7, 1929. Copies deposited November 8, 1929. The first edition may be identified by the words "First Edition" and the code letters I-D (September, 1929) on the verso of the title-page.

On a paper ribbon issued with the book there is the statement that this book contains the group of seven poems "From a Very Little Sphinx," hitherto unpublished in book form. This statement is erroneous. All seven poems in "From a Very Little Sphinx" had been included in *American Poetry 1925: A Miscellany,* and one, under the title "The Cheerful Abstainer" had been included earlier in *The Bowling Green: An Anthology of Verse* (1924). No part of the contents of the volume presently collated is new.

CONTENTS

Part One	
From a very little Sphinx	
Afternoon on a Hill	Renascence
City Trees	Second April
The Blue Flag in the Bog	" "
Journey	" "
Eel-Grass	" "
God's World	Renascence
Pastoral	Second April
Assault	" "
Low-Tide	" "
Song of a Second April	" "
Inland	" "
Doubt No More that Oberon	" "
Exiled	" "
Alms	" "
Autumn Chant	Harp-Weaver
Nuit Blanche	"

Bibliography

The Wood Road	Harp-Weaver
The Spring and the Fall	"

Part Two

First Fig	Few Figs
Second Fig	" "
To the Not Impossible Him	" "
Recuerdo	" "
The Unexplorer	" "
Grown-Up	" "
Daphne	" "
The Philosopher	" "
Travel	Second April
Rosemary	" "
Ebb	" "
The Little Hill	" "
Wild Swans	
Sorrow	Renascence
Elaine	Second April
Souvenir	Harp-Weaver
Scrub	"
Departure	"
The Curse	
The Little Ghost	Renascence

Part Three

Renascence	Renascence

Part Four

Portrait by a Neighbor	Few Figs
The Bean-Stalk	Second April
Wraith	" "
Lament	" "
Tavern	Renascence
When the Year Grows Old	"
The Return from Town	Harp-Weaver
The Ballad of the Harp-Weaver	"

Part Five

Memorial to D. C.	Second April
Epitaph	" "
Prayer to Persephone	" "
Chorus	" "
Elegy	" "
Dirge	" "

[125]

Edna St. Vincent Millay

Part Six—Sonnets

40. POEMS SELECTED FOR YOUNG PEOPLE, Limited: 1929

Title-page similar to that of trade edition, except that second and third lines and date are in green.

Collation: Pp. xiv + 114, consisting of, after decorated end-sheet and one blank leaf not counted in pagination; p.[i] bastard title (verso blank); p.[iii] bibliographical note (verso blank); p.[v] blank (frontispiece tipped to verso); p.[vii] title-page as above (copyright on verso); pp.[ix-x] illustrations; pp.[xi-xiii] [*misnumbered* vii-ix], *Contents;* p.[xiv] blank; through remainder of book the collation is similar to that of the trade edition, except that there is only one blank page following the text.

8vo, size 6⅜ x 9¾. Binding of gray-green boards, white linen back. Covers blank. Cream paper label on backbone, lettered as backbone of trade edition. Top uncut, fore edge deckle, lower edge rough trimmed.

This edition was published simultaneously with the trade edition and bears the words "First Edition" and the code letters I-D on the verso of the title-page. The bibliographical note on p.[III] reads: Of the first edition of Edna St. Vincent Millay's Poems Selected for Young People one thousand and fifty copies have been printed on Arches hand-made paper. Only one thousand copies are for sale. This volume is number [*here number is entered in ink*].

41.   TWICE REQUIRED: 1931

Twice Required | By | Edna St. Vincent Millay | [*publishers' seal*] | Harper & Brothers Publishers | New York and London | MCMXXXI

All the above in upper and lower case, words "Publishers" and "and" in italic. First line and seal in green.

Collation: Pp. VI + 6, consisting of pp.[I-II] blank; p.[III] title-page as above (publication notice in a box on verso); p.[v] *Synopsis* (synopsis continued on verso); pp. 1-3, text; pp.[4-6] blank.

8vo, size 5½ x 8⅛. Binding of heather boards. Covers blank. Backstrip, on paper label, first three lines in capitals, rest upper and lower case: [*three rules*] | twice | re- | quired [*device*] | Edna | St. Vincent | Millay | [*rule*] | Harpers [*three rules*]. Customary dummy construction practice was followed, and it will be noted that there are no endsheets as in a complete book, and the backstrip is pasted on the back cover.

I choose to include a full collation of this dummy, not so much because of the first appearance within their own covers of three of the sonnets which later appeared in *Fatal Interview*, but because of the change of title. Fifty of these dummies were made up, but not all of them were sent out for advertising purposes, and of those that did leave Harpers, the majority were recalled and destroyed. There are probably half a dozen in existence.

Contents, with the number of each sonnet as printed in *Fatal Interview*:
XI. Not in a silver casket cool with pearls

Edna St. Vincent Millay

XXVI. Women have loved before as I love now
XXXI. When we that wore the myrtle wear the dust.

42.   FATAL INTERVIEW: 1931

Fatal Interview | Sonnets | By | Edna St. Vincent Millay |
[*publishers' seal*] | Harper & Brothers Publishers | New
York and London | MCMXXXI
> *First letter of each of first two words, seal, and date in
> red. First, second, and sixth lines and word "Publishers" in
> upper and lower case; rest in capitals; words "Sonnets", "Pub-
> lishers", and "and" in italic.*

Collation: Pp. xii + 52, consisting of, after endsheet; p.[i]
bastard title (quotation from Donne on verso); p.[iii] title-
page as above (copyright on verso); p.[v] list of books (verso
blank); p.[vii] dedication (verso blank); pp. ix-x, Contents;
p.[xi] half-title (verso blank); pp. 1-52, text; endsheet.

16mo, size 5½ x 8⅜. Binding of heather boards, black cloth
back and corners. Covers blank. Backbone: [*three rules*] |
Fatal | Inter- | view | [*device*] | Edna | St. Vincent | Millay |
[*rule*] | Harpers | [*three rules*]. The foregoing on a white
paper label, first three lines in capitals, rest upper and lower
case, with last line in italic. All edges trimmed. Also bound in
blue limp leather, front cover blind-stamp ruled into six
panels, with gold figure of harp player in center. Backbone
lettered in gold capitals: [*blind rule*] | FATAL | INTER- | VIEW |
[*gold rule*] | EDNA | ST. VINCENT | MILLAY | [*blind rule*] | [*gold
ornament*] | HARPERS | [*blind rule*]. Back cover blank. Top
edge gilt. Fore and lower edges rough trimmed.

Published April 15, 1931. Copies deposited the same day. Different
bindings issued simultaneously. The first edition may be identified
by the words "First Edition" and the code letters C-F (March, 1931)
on the verso of the title-page. Some copies of the boards binding
have yellow stained tops. The entire edition was to have been

Bibliography

stained, but at the request of the author the staining was discontinued after 500 or less had been so treated. It is believed that the stained copies were the first bound, but it is not known whether the stained copies were the first distributed. A misprint of "than" for "that" in the fourth line on p. 47 appears in all copies of the first edition: this was corrected in a later edition, on June 30, 1931.

Originally the title of this book was announced as *Twice Required* (cf. Collation No. 41), words taken from the second line of the fourteenth sonnet, which reads "Since of no creature living the last breath is twice required," but the opportunity of using the publication of this book as a commemoration of the three hundredth anniversary of the death of John Donne was too fine to be overlooked. The quotation from Donne on the verso of the bastard title is:

> By our first strange and fatall interview,
> By all desires which thereof did ensue.

Contents: First book printing for all these sonnets. The poems which had appeared in the dummy of *Twice Required* are marked with an asterisk.

What thing is this that, built of salt and lime
This beast that rends me in the sight of all
No lack of counsel from the shrewd and wise
Nay, learned doctor, these fine leeches fresh
Of all that ever in extreme disease
Since I cannot persuade you from this mood
Night is my sister, and how deep in love
Yet in an hour to come, disdainful dust
When you are dead, and your disturbing eyes
Strange thing that I, by nature nothing prone
* Not in a silver casket cool with pearls
Olympian gods, mark now my bedside lamp
I said, seeing how the winter gale increased
Since of no creature living the last breath
My worship from this hour the Sparrow-Drawn
I dreamed I moved among Elysian fields
Sweet love, sweet thorn, when lightly to my heart
Shall I be prisoner till my pulses stop
My most distinguished guest and learned friend
Think not, nor for a moment let your mind
Gone in good sooth you are: not even in a dream

Now by this moon, before this moon shall wane
I know the face of falsehood and her tongue
Whereas at morning in a jeweled crown
Peril upon the paths of this desire
* Women have loved before as I love now
Moon, that against the lintel of the west
When we are old and these rejoicing veins
Heart, have no pity on this house of bone
Love is not all; it is not meat nor drink
* When we that wore the myrtle wear the dust
Time, that is pleased to lengthen out the day
Sorrowful dreams remembered after waking
Most wicked words, forbear to speak them out
Clearly my ruined garden as it stood
Hearing your words, and not a word among them
Believe, if ever the bridges of this town
You say: "Since life is cruel enough at best"
Love me no more, now let the god depart
You loved me not at all, but let it go
I said in the beginning, did I not
O ailing love, compose your struggling wing
Summer, be seen no more within this wood
If to be left were to be left alone
I know my mind and I have made my choice
Even in the moment of our earliest kiss
Well, I have lost you; and I lost you fairly
Now by the path I climbed, I journey back
There is a well into whose bottomless eye
The heart once broken is a heart no more
If in the years to come you should recall
Oh, sleep forever in the Latmian cave

43. FATAL INTERVIEW, Limited:

1931

Title-page identical with that of the trade edition.

Collation: Pp. xiv + 54, consisting of, after blue-gray end-sheet; p.[i] bastard title (bibliographical note on verso);

Bibliography

p.[III] blank; p.[IV] quotation from Donne; p.[V] title-page as above (copyright on verso); p.[VII] list of books (verso blank); p.[IX] dedication (verso blank); pp. XI-XII, *Contents;* p.[XIII] half-title (verso blank); pp. 1-52, text; pp.[53-54] blank; endsheet. Tipped in between p.[II] and p.[III] is a leaf of Japan vellum, recto of which reads: Of the first edition of "Fatal Interview", this is copy number [*here follows number and signature in ink*]. Verso of this leaf blank.

16mo, size 6 x 9¼. Binding of blue-gray boards, white cloth back. Covers blank. Backbone: [*wavy rule*] | Fatal | Inter- | view | Sonnets | by | Edna | St. Vincent | Millay | [*dotted rule*] | Harpers | [*wavy rule*]. The foregoing on a paper label, first three and last lines in capitals, rest upper and lower case, the fourth and fifth lines in italic. Top and fore edges uncut. Lower edge rough trimmed.

The verso of the title-page bears the words "First Edition" and the code letters C-F. There is no precedence among the three editions of this book: the two limited editions were published simultaneously with the trade edition.

The bibliographical note on p.[II] reads: This first edition of Fatal Interview set up and printed from type, consists of five hundred and fifteen copies, each numbered and signed by the author. Thirty-six copies are printed on Japan vellum, of which only the first thirty-one copies are for sale. Four hundred and seventy-nine copies are printed on Arches hand-made paper, of which only numbers thirty-seven to five hundred and five are for sale The type has been destroyed.

JAPAN VELLUM EDITION

The ultra-limited edition of thirty-six copies on Japan vellum differs from the foregoing only in the stock on which it is printed and in the binding. The endsheets are light gray, the binding is of gray boards with vellum back and corners. There is a leather label on the backbone, lettered in gold capitals: [*rule*] | FATAL | INTER- | VIEW | [*device*] | MILLAY | [*rule*] | HARPERS.

44. FATAL INTERVIEW, English: 1931

Fatal Interview | Sonnets | By | Edna St. Vincent Millay | "By our first strange and fatall interview, | By all desires which thereof did ensue." | —John Donne | [*publisher's monogram*] | Hamish Hamilton | 90 Great Russell Street London

There is no date on the title-page. First, third, and seventh to ninth lines in capitals, rest upper and lower case; second, fifth and sixth lines in italic.

Collation: Pp. 64 consisting of, after endsheet; pp.[1-2] blank; p.[3] bastard title (list of books on verso); p.[5] title-page as above (verso printer's notice); p.[7] dedication (verso blank); pp. 9-10, *Contents;* p.[11] half-title (verso blank); pp. 13-64, text; endsheet.

8vo, size $4\frac{7}{8}$ x $7\frac{5}{8}$. Bound in purple cloth. Covers blank. Backbone lettered in gold capitals: FATAL | INTER- | VIEW | EDNA | ST. VINCENT | MILLAY | HAMISH | HAMILTON. All edges trimmed.

Published in April, 1931, subsequent to the American edition. The contents are the same as in the American edition.

45. FATAL INTERVIEW, Lutetia Type: 1931

Fatal Interview | Sonnets | by | Edna St. Vincent Millay | [*publishers' seal*] | Harper & Brothers Publishers | New York and London | 1931

Second line in capitals, rest upper and lower case, fifth and sixth lines in italic. First line and date in red. Seal on light buff square.

Bibliography

Collation: Pp. XII + 56, consisting of, after marbled end-sheet; pp.[I-II] blank; p.[III] bastard title (quotation from Donne on verso) ; p.[V] title-page as above (list of books and copyright on verso) ; p.[VII] dedication (verso blank) ; pp.[IX-XI] *Contents*; p.[XII] blank; pp. 1-52, text; p.[53] colophon; pp.[54-56] blank; endsheet.

16mo, size 3¼ x 4⅝. Bound in full green calf, gold-stamped on backstrip: FATAL | INTER- | VIEW | MILLAY. All edges gilt. The code letters h-f (August, 1931) are at the foot of the copyright page.

The text of the colophon is as follows: This edition of "Fatal Interview" is set in Lutetia Italic type designed by J. von Krimpen and cast under his supervision at the ancient foundry of J. Enschede en Zonen in Haarlem, Holland. Composition by A. W. Rushmore at The Golden Hind Press, Madison, N. J. Printed on Pannekoek, Dutch, mouldmade paper by the Haddon Craftsmen, Camden, N. J. Binding by Sangorski and Sutcliffe of London.

Before the leather bound copies were received in this country from London, there were bound up a half dozen copies in marbled boards with black cloth back and paper label on the backstrip, which copies were for exhibition purposes and were not for sale. In either binding this book is a gem.

46. THE PRINCESS MARRIES THE PAGE: 1932

The Princess | Marries the Page | A play in one act | by | Edna St. Vincent Millay | Decorations by | J. Paget-Fredericks | [*publishers' seal*] | Harper & Brothers Publishers | New York and London | 1932

All the above is set within an ornamental border in brown; seal and date also in brown. Third and fourth lines in roman capitals; fifth line in upper and lower case roman; all rest in upper and lower case italic.

[133]

Edna ·St. Vincent Millay

Collation: Pp. XIV + 56, consisting of, after gray-green end-sheet and one blank leaf not counted in pagination; p.[I] bastard title (list of books on verso) ; p.[III] title-page as above (copyright on verso) ; p.[V] dedication (decoration on verso) ; pp. VII-IX, *Note;* p.[X] blank; pp. XI-XII, *Preface;* p.[XIII] half-title (verso blank) ; pp. 1-[51], text; p.[52] colophon; pp.[53-56] blank; endsheet. Tipped in between p.[II] and p.[III] is a leaf of glazed paper with a colored frontispiece on verso; recto blank. The following leaves are parts of signatures, but are not numbered or counted in the pagination: one leaf between pp. 2 and 3 carrying facsimiles of musical manuscript by Deems Taylor on both sides; three leaves with illustration on rectos, versos blank, between pp. 8 and 9, pp. 24 and 25, and pp. 36 and 37, respectively.

8vo, size 6½ x 9⅜. Binding of dark green boards, yellow cloth back. Covers blank. Backbone: [*devices*] THE PRINCESS MAR-RIES THE PAGE [*device*] MILLAY [*devices*] HARPERS [*devices*]. The foregoing stamped in gold, upper and lower case, reading from top to bottom. All edges trimmed. Also bound in blue limp leather, front cover blind-stamp ruled into six panels, with gold figure of harp player in center. Backbone lettered in gold capitals: THE | PRINCESS | MARRIES | THE | PAGE | [*gold rule*] | EDNA | ST. VINCENT | MILLAY | [*blind rule*] | [*gold ornament*] | HARPERS | [*blind rule*]. Back cover blank. Top edge gilt. Fore and lower edges rough trimmed.

Published October 19, 1932. Copies deposited October 20, 1932. Different bindings issued simultaneously. The first edition may be identified by the words "First Edition" on the verso of the title-page; there are no code letters. The text of the colophon is as follows: Set by hand in Weiss Antiqua Type by Arthur and Edna Rushmore at the Golden Hind Press Madison New Jersey Mcmxxxii.

Bibliography

47. THE PRINCESS MARRIES THE PAGE, English: 1932

The Princess | Marries the Page | A Play in One Act | By | Edna St. Vincent Millay | Decorations by | J. Paget-Fredericks | [*publishers' monogram*] | Publishers | Hamish Hamilton, Ltd. | 90 Great Russell Street, London | 1932
Title-page similar to that of American edition. Eighth and ninth lines in capitals. Date in black.

Collation and size are the same as those of the American edition. Bound in purple cloth. Backbone lettered in gold capitals: THE | PRIN- | CESS | MARRIES | THE | PAGE | EDNA | ST. | VINCENT | MILLAY | HAMISH | HAMILTON. Back cover blank. Top and fore edges trimmed, lower edge rough trimmed. This English edition, issued after the American edition, contains the same sheets as the American edition, only the title-page having been altered.

48. THE PRINCESS MARRIES THE PAGE, Baker: 1934

The Princess | Marries the Page | A Play in One Act | By | Edna St. Vincent Millay | [*publishers' seal*] | Special Edition | Made for the Walter H. Baker Company | by | Harper & Brothers | Publishers
There is no date on the title-page. Title-page similar to that of trade edition, except all in black, and last five lines in upper and lower case italic.

Collation: Pp. x [*misnumbered* XII] + 52, consisting of; p.[I] title-page as above (copyright on verso); p.[III] dedication (list of books on verso); pp.[V-VII] [*misnumbered* VII-IX], *Note;* p.[VIII] blank; pp.[IX-X] [*misnumbered* XI-XII], *Preface;*

pp. 1-[51], text; p.[52] colophon. Between pp. 2 and 3 is a leaf which is an integral part of a signature, but is not numbered or counted in the pagination, carrying facsimiles of musical manuscript by Deems Taylor on both sides.

8vo, size 5 x 7¼. Binding of light blue-gray wrappers. Front cover: A Play in One Act By | Edna St. Vincent Millay | [*two rules*] | The Princess | Marries The Page | Walter H. Baker Co., Boston. The foregoing within a double rule box, second line in italic upper and lower case, rest in roman capitals. Back cover and backbone blank. All edges trimmed.

As the code letters B-I on the verso of the title-page indicate, this edition (of 2500 copies) was printed in February, 1934. The plates of the regular trade edition (cf. Collation No. 46) were used, but the size of the page was reduced. and the illustrations and the bastard title were omitted. In other respects the text of this acting edition is the same as the text of the original edition.

49. WINE FROM THESE GRAPES: 1934

Wine | From These Grapes | by | Edna St. Vincent Millay | [*publishers' seal*] | Harper & Brothers Publishers | New York and London | MCMXXXIV

First letter of each word in title, publishers' seal, and date in red. Third and fourth lines, and words "Harper & Brothers" in capitals; rest upper and lower case, words "Publishers" and "and" being in italic.

Collation: Pp. x + 94, consisting of, after endsheet; p.[I] bastard title (list of books on verso) ; p.[III] title-page as above (copyright on verso) ; p.[V] quotation from *The Buck in the Snow* (verso blank) ; pp. VII-VIII, *Contents;* p.[IX] half-title (verso blank) ; p.[1] divisional number I (verso blank) ; pp. 3-13, text of Part I; p.[14] blank; p.[15] divisional number II (verso blank) ; pp. 17-25, text of Part II; p.[26] blank; p.[27]

Bibliography

divisional number III (verso blank); pp. 29-31, text of Part III; p.[32] blank; p.[33] divisional number IV (verso blank); pp. 35-54, text of Part IV; p.[55] divisional number V and *Epitaph for the Race of Man* (verso blank); pp. 57-91, text of Part V; pp.[92-94] blank; endsheet. Verso of every leaf in Part V also blank.

8vo, size 5¼ x 8⅜. Binding of gray-green boards, black cloth back and corners. Covers blank. Backbone: [*three rules*] | Wine | From | These | Grapes | [*device*] | Edna | St. Vincent | Millay | [*rule*] | Harpers | [*three rules*]. The foregoing on a paper label, first four lines in capitals, rest upper and lower case, last line in italic. Top edge trimmed, fore and lower edges rough trimmed. Also bound in blue limp leather, front cover blind-stamp ruled into six panels, with gold figure of harp player in center. Backbone lettered in gold capitals: [*blind rule*] | WINE | FROM | THESE | GRAPES |[*gold rule*] | EDNA | ST. VINCENT | MILLAY | [*blind rule*] | [*gold ornaments*] | HARPERS | [*blind rule*]. Back cover blank. Top edge gilt. Fore and lower edges rough trimmed.

Published November 1, 1934. Copies deposited November 2, 1934. The first edition may be identified by the words "First Edition" and the code letters I-I (September, 1934) on the verso of the title. Different bindings issued simultaneously. The publishers' dummy of this book, made up about two months in advance of publication for the use of salesmen, contains three sonnets included in the published volume. These sonnets are double starred in the following list of contents.

Contents, first book printing for all poems:
    Wine From These Grapes

I
The Return
October—An Etching
Autumn Daybreak
The Oak-Leaves
The Fledgling
The Hedge of Hemlocks

Edna St. Vincent Millay

Cap D'Antibes
From a Train Window
The Fawn

II
Valentine
In the Grave No Flower
Childhood Is the Kingdom Where Nobody Dies
The Solid Sprite Who Stands Alone
Spring in the Garden
Sonnet (Time, that renews the tissues of this frame)

III
Aubade
Sappho Crosses the Dark River into Hades

IV
Epitaph
On Thought in Harness
Desolation Dreamed Of
The Leaf and the Tree
** On the Wide Heath
Apostrophe to Man
Two Sonnets in Memory
    (I   As men have loved their lovers in times past)
    (II Where can the heart be hidden in the ground)
My Spirit, Sore From Marching
Conscientious Objector
Above These Cares
If Still Your Orchards Bear
Lines for a Grave-stone
How Naked, How without a Wall

V
    Epitaph for the Race of Man
** Before this cooling planet shall be cold
When Death was young and bleaching bones were few
Cretaceous bird, your giant claw no lime
O Earth, unhappy planet born to die
When Man is gone and only gods remain
** See where Capella with her golden kids
He heard the coughing tiger in the night
Observe how Mujanoshita cracked in two
He woke in terror to a sky more bright

Bibliography

The broken dike, the levee washed away
Sweeter was loss than silver coins to spend
Now forth to meadow as the farmer goes
His heatless room the watcher of the stars
Him not the golden fang of furious heaven
Now sets his foot upon the eastern sill
Alas for Man, so stealthily betrayed
Only the diamond and the diamond's dust
Here lies, and none to mourn him but the sea

50. WINE FROM THESE GRAPES, Limited: 1934

Wine | From These Grapes | By | Edna St. Vincent Millay | [*row of asterisks*] | [*publishers' seal*] | [*row of asterisks*] | Harper & Brothers Publishers | New York and London | 1934

Above is title-page of first volume of two volume set. All upper and lower case, first to third, and fifth lines in italic. First two lines, asterisks, seal, and date in brown.

Collation: Pp. xiv + 54, consisting of, after endsheet; pp.[i-ii] blank; p.[iii] bastard title (verso blank); p.[v] bibliographical note (list of books on verso); p.[vii] title-page as above (copyright on verso); p.[ix] quotation from *The Buck in the Snow* (verso blank); pp.[xi-xii], *Table of Contents;* p.[xiii] half-title (verso blank); p.[1] divisional number I (verso blank); pp. 3-13, text of Part I; p.[14] blank; p.[15] divisional number II (verso blank); pp. 17-25, text of Part II; p.[26] blank; p.[27] divisional number III (verso blank); pp. 29-31, text of Part III; p.[32] blank; p.[33] divisional number IV (verso blank); pp. 35-54, text of Part IV; endsheet.

8vo, size 6⅝ x 10. Binding of blue boards, white linen back. Covers blank. Backbone: [*fancy rule; plain rule*] | Wine | From | These | Grapes | [*asterisk*] | Edna | St. | Vincent | Millay | [*rule*] | Harpers | [*plain rule; fancy rule*]. **The fore-**

going on a paper label, last line in capitals, rest in upper and lower case, the author's name being in italic. Top and fore edges uncut, lower edge trimmed.

The bibliographical note on p.[v] reads: This first edition of Wine From These Grapes consists of two volumes Wine From These Grapes and Epitaph for the Race of Man. Three hundred and thirty-five sets have been printed and the type distributed. The first volume of each set is numbered and signed by the author. Thirty-six sets are printed on Japan vellum of which only the first thirty-one are for sale. Two hundred and ninety-nine sets are printed on Worthy Charta paper of which only numbers thirty-seven to three hundred and twenty-five are for sale.

Tipped in between p.[IV] and p.[v] is a leaf of Japan vellum, recto of which reads: Of the first edition of Wine from These Grapes and Epitaph for the Race of Man this set is no.. [here follows number and signature in ink]. Verso of this leaf is blank.

This volume contains the same material as Parts I to IV inclusive of the trade edition, and was published simultaneously therewith, on November 1, 1934. The words "First Edition" are on the verso of the title-page.

VOLUME TWO

Epitaph for | The Race of Man | By | Edna St. Vincent Millay | [row of asterisks] | [publishers' seal] | [row of asterisks] | Harper & Brothers Publishers | New York and London | 1934

Above is title-page of second volume of two volume set. Typography like that of title-page of first volume, supra.

Collation: Pp. XII + 40, consisting of, after endsheet; pp.[I-II] blank; p.[III] bastard title (verso blank); p.[v] bibliographical note as in first volume (verso blank); p.[VII] title-page as above (copyright on verso); p.[IX], *Table of Contents* (verso blank); p.[XI] half-title (verso blank); pp. 1-35, text; p.[36] blank; p.[37] colophon; pp.[38-40] blank; endsheet. Verso of every leaf of text is unnumbered and blank.

Size and binding identical with first volume. Backbone:

Bibliography

[fancy rule; plain rule] | Epitaph | for the | Race of | Man |
[asterisk] | Edna | St. | Vincent | Millay | *[rule]* | Harpers |
[plain rule; fancy rule]. The foregoing on a paper label,
typography like that of first volume.

The colophon on p.[37] reads: This Limited First Edition of *Wine
From These Grapes* is hand-set by Arthur and Edna Rushmore at
The Golden Hind Press, Madison, New Jersey, in Lutetia type from
the foundry of Joh. Enschedé en Zonen, Haarlem, Holland. Printed
by The Harbor Press in New York City. Published by Harper &
Brothers, New York and London. October MCMXXXIV.

This volume contains the same material as Part V of the trade
edition, and accompanied by the first volume, was published simultaneously therewith.

Japan Vellum Edition

The ultra-limited edition of 36 copies on Japan vellum, in two
volumes, differs from the foregoing only in the stock on which it is
printed, the size, and the binding. The size is 7 x 11. The binding
is of light blue gray boards, with vellum back and corners. The
backbones are stamped in gold, with the title of each volume (one
line) and the author's name (one line) lettered from bottom to
top within ornamental brackets in gold; the publishers' name is
lettered horizontally at the foot of the backbone in gold. The ultra-
limited edition was also published simultaneously with the trade
edition.

51. WINE FROM THESE GRAPES,
English: 1934

Wine From These | Grapes | By | Edna St. Vincent Millay
| *[publisher's monogram]* | Hamish Hamilton | 90 Great
Russell Street London
  *There is no date on the title-page. Author's name upper
and lower case; all rest in capitals.*

Collation: Pp. 80, consisting of, after endsheet; p.[1] bastard
title (list of books on verso) ; p.[3] title-page as above (verso:

Edna St. Vincent Millay

First published 1934) ; p.[5] quotation from *The Buck in the Snow* (verso blank) ; pp. 7-8, *Contents;* p.[9] half-title (verso blank) ; p.[11] divisional number I (verso blank) ; pp. 13-22, text of Part I; p.[23] divisional number II (verso blank) ; pp. 25-32, text of Part II; p.[33] divisional number III (verso blank) ; pp. 35-37, text of Part III; p.[38] blank; p.[39] divisional number IV (verso blank) ; pp. 41-57, text of Part IV; p.[58] blank; p.[59] divisional number V *Epitaph for the Race of Man* (verso blank) ; pp. 61-[78] text of Part V; pp. 79-80, blank; endsheet.

8vo, size 4¾ x 7⅝. Bound in dark blue cloth. Covers blank. Backbone lettered in gold capitals: WINE | FROM | THESE | GRAPES | EDNA | ST. | VINCENT | MILLAY | HAMISH | HAMILTON. All edges trimmed.

Published in November, 1934, subsequent to the American edition. The contents are the same as the American edition.

52.   FLOWERS OF EVIL: 1936

Flowers Of Evil | From the French of | Charles Baudelaire | By | George Dillon | [*asterisk*] | Edna St. Vincent Millay | With the Original Texts | and with a Preface by | Miss Millay | [*publishers' seal*] | Harper & Brothers Publishers | New York 1936 London

All the above set within a border of four rules in green. First line in italic capitals; fourth, seventh, and eighth lines in italic upper and lower case; ninth line in roman upper and lower case; rest in roman capitals.

Collation: Pp. XL + 286, consisting of, after marbled endsheet and one blank leaf not counted in pagination; p.[I] bastard title (lists of books on verso) ; p.[III] title-page as above (copyright on verso) ; pp. V-XXXIV, *Preface;* p.[XXXV] blank; pp. XXXVI-XXXIX, *Contents;* p. [XL] blank; p.[1] half-title; pp. 2-265, text; p.[266] blank; pp. 267-278, biographical note;

pp. 279-282, index; p.[283] colophon; pp.[284-286] blank;
endsheet. P.[268] is also blank.

8vo, size 5¾ x 8⅝. Bound in black cloth. Covers blank. Back-
bone: [*four rules*] | Flowers | Of | Evil | From the French of |
Charles Baudelaire | By | George | Dillon | [*asterisk*] | Edna
St. Vincent | Millay | [*rule*] | Harpers | [*four rules*]. The fore-
going on a gold paper label printed in black, first three and
last lines in capitals, rest upper and lower case, fourth and
sixth lines being in italic. Top and lower edges trimmed.
Fore edge rough trimmed.

Published April 2, 1936. Copies deposited March 31, 1936. The
first edition may be identified by the words "First Edition" and the
code letters B-L (February, 1936), on the verso of the title-page.
Set in Intertype Walbaum and printed on Flemish Book Paper, with
format by A. W. Rushmore.

53. FLOWERS OF EVIL, English:
1936

Flowers of Evil | From the French of | Charles Baudelaire |
By | George Dillon | [*asterisk*] | Edna St. Vincent Millay |
With the Original Texts | and with a Preface by | Miss
Millay | [*publishers' monogram*] | Publishers | Hamish
Hamilton Ltd. | 90 Great Russell Street, London

*There is no date on the title-page, which differs from that
of the American edition only in the alteration of the publishers' monogram and imprint.*

Collation and size are the same as those of the American
edition, and the binding is very similar. The English has a
slight difference in the texture of the cloth; two blind rules
have been added at the top and bottom of the backstrip respectively; and the last line of the paper label reads "Hamish
Hamilton" instead of "Harpers". This English edition contains the same sheets as the American edition, only the title
page having been altered.

Edna St. Vincent Millay

54.   CONVERSATION AT
MIDNIGHT

SECTION II

APPEARANCES and MUSIC

a. APPEARANCES

Anthology of Magazine Verse for 1914, by William Stanley Braithwaite. Issued by W. S. B., Cambridge, Massachusetts. First book printing of "The Shroud" on p. 72, with credit line to *The Forum* (for October, 1914).

A Book of Vassar Verse. Published by the *Vassar Miscellany*, 1916. (Poughkeepsie, New York.) Published December 13, 1916. Contributions to this anthology of Vassar College poetry, reprints from the *Vassar Miscellany Monthly*, 1894-1916, consist of three poems, here first printed in book form; "Interim" on p. 81, 207 lines, and "The Suicide" on p. 126, 138 lines, and "Why Did I Ever Come to This Place?" on p. 163, 73 lines. The last poem has never been reprinted. The first two poems were amplified by a few lines each for their inclusion in *Renascence* later.

The New Poetry: An Anthology. Edited by Harriet Monroe and Alice Corbin Henderson, Editors of *Poetry*. New York, Macmillan, 1917. Published February 28, 1917. First book printing of "God's World" on p. 225, with credit to *The Forum* for July, 1913, and of "Ashes of Life" on p. 226 with credit to *The Forum* (for August, 1915). Also contains "The Shroud."

The Melody of Earth: An Anthology of Garden and Nature Poems. Selected by Mrs. Waldo Richards. Boston, Houghton, 1918. Published March 28, 1918. Contains "The End of Summer" on p. 49, 12 lines, which is the only appearance of this poem, as far as I can discover. Also contains "Afternoon on a Hill" and "The Little Ghost."

Anthology of Magazine Verse for 1919 and Year Book

of American Poetry. Edited by William Stanley Braith-waite. Boston, Small, Maynard. Published December 15, 1919. First book printing of "She Is Overheard Singing" on p. 63, with credit to *Poetry* for May, 1919, and of "Elaine" on p. 70, with credit to *The Nation* for November 16, 1918.

ANTHOLOGY OF MAGAZINE VERSE FOR 1920 and Year Book of American Poetry. Edited by William Stanley Braith-waite. Boston, Small, Maynard. Published November 8, 1920. First book printing of "Departure" on p. 35, with credit to *Ainslee's Magazine* (for August, 1919), and of "Inland" on p. 67, with credit to *Ainslee's Magazine* (for November, 1919), and of "Exiled" on p. 94, with credit to *Ainslee's Magazine* (for December, 1919), and of "Elegy Before Death" on p. 111, with credit to *Ainslee's Magazine* (for January, 1920).

FIFTY CONTEMPORARY ONE ACT PLAYS, by Frank Shay and Pierre Loving. Cincinnati, Stewart and Kidd. Published January 6, 1921, copies deposited January 10, 1921. First book printing of "Aria da Capo" on pp. 433-441. Contains the text alone, without the author's suggestions.

STAR POINTS. Selected by Mrs. Waldo Richards. Boston, Houghton. Published March 16, 1921. First book printing of "Travel" on p. 158, with acknowledgment to Miss Millay personally. Also contains "The Little Tavern" on p. 63, which is the same as "Tavern" that appeared in *Renascence*.

THE PROVINCETOWN PLAYS. Edited and selected by George Cram Cook and Frank Shay. Cincinnati, Stewart Kidd. Published April 11, 1921. Contains "Aria da Capo" on pp. 45-69.

Bibliography

FOLK SONGS OF MANY PEOPLES WITH ENGLISH VERSIONS BY AMERICAN POETS. Compiled and edited by Florence Hudson Botsford. The Woman's Press, New York City. Published June 24, 1921. Volume I of this two-volume set contains the following: p. 6, "Wedding Joy", an Esthonian folk dance with English version by Miss Millay, 12 lines; p. 34, "Sowing the Rue", a Lithuanian folk song with English version by Miss Millay, 14 lines; p. 71, "Why, Oh Mother?", a Polish song with paraphrase by Miss Millay, 35 lines; p. 151, "The Disappointed Suitors", a Slovak folk song with paraphrase by Miss Millay, 16 lines. The original, the translation, and the music are given in each instance.

MODERN AMERICAN POETRY (Revised and enlarged edition), by Louis Untermeyer. New York, Harcourt, 1921. Published July 18, 1921. First book printing of the sonnet "Pity me not because the light of day" on p. 382, and of the sonnet "I shall go back again to the bleak shore" on p. 383, and of "Wild Swans" on p. 383, and of "The Pear Tree" on p. 383. The last poem, as far as I can discover, has never appeared in any of Miss Millay's books, but has appeared in revisions of the Untermeyer anthology. The first binding does not have gilt rule at foot of backstrip.

POEMS OF THE DANCE: An Anthology [1500 B.C.-1920 A.D.]. Chosen and edited by Edward R. Dickson. New York, Alfred A. Knopf, 1921. Published November 1, 1921. First book printing of the sonnet "How healthily their feet upon the floor" on p. 169, here under the title of "The Dance."

ANTHOLOGY OF MAGAZINE VERSE FOR 1921 and Year Book of American Poetry. Edited by William Stanley Braithwaite. Boston, Small, Maynard. Published November 9,

Edna St. Vincent Millay

1921. First book printing of the sonnet "I see so clearly now my similar years" on p. 116, with credit to *The Century* (for March, 1921). Also contains "Passer Mortuus Est" on p. 114 and "To a poet that died young" on p. 115.

POETICA EROTICA: A Collection of Rare and Curious Amatory Verse. Edited by T. R. Smith. Published for subscribers only by Boni and Liveright, New York, 1921. Volume Two of the three-volume set contains first book printing of "The Betrothal" on p. 302, and of the sonnet "I, being born a woman and distressed" on p. 303.

WALT WHITMAN IN MICKLE STREET, by Elizabeth Keller. Kennerley, New York, 1921. On the dust wrapper and also on the half-title appears the last line of the poem "Ashes of Life". This is not a first, but an interesting, printing. In each copy of the book was a prospectus of Millay books, to be used as a bookmark.

A LITTLE ANTHOLOGY OF VERY SHORT POEMS FROM THE MAGAZINES OF 1921. (Done by the Bookfellows at the Torch Press, Cedar Rapids, Iowa.) First book printing of "The Hungry Heart" on p. 38, with credit to *Vanity Fair* (for February, 1921).

AMERICAN POETRY 1922: A MISCELLANY. New York, Harcourt, Brace & Company. Published September 7, 1922. First book printing for eight sonnets on pp. 193 ff. "When you that at this moment are to me", "What's this of death from you who will never die", "I know I am but summer to your heart", "Here is a wound that never will heal I know", "What lips my lips have kissed, and where, and why", "Euclid alone has looked on beauty bare", "Oh, oh, you will be sorry for that word", "Say what you will and scratch my heart to find."

Bibliography

CONTEMPORARY POETRY. Edited by Marguerite Wilkinson. New York, Macmillan, 1923. Published June 19, 1923. First book printing for "Autumn Chant" on p. 212.

THE BOWLING GREEN: An Anthology of Verse. Selected by Christopher Morley. Garden City, Doubleday, Page & Company, 1924. First book printing for "The Cheerful Abstainer" on p. 114, which later became the fourth of the seven poems "From a Very Little Sphinx" in *American Poetry, 1925, A Miscellany* and again in *Poems Selected for Young People.*

AMERICAN POETRY 1925: A MISCELLANY. New York, Harcourt, Brace & Company. Published September 3, 1925. First book printing for all but the fourth of the group of poems entitled "From a Very Little Sphinx," on pp. 139 ff.

MAY DAYS: An Anthology of Verse from Masses-Liberator. Chosen and edited by Genevieve Taggard, with woodcuts by J. J. Lankes. Boni & Liveright, New York, MCMXXV. Published December 4, 1925. First book printing of "To the Liberty Bell" on p. 187. This poem appeared in *Liberator* for October, 1922, and has not been reprinted in book form elsewhere.

THE BEST POEMS OF 1925. Selected by Thomas Moult and decorated by John Austen. New York, Harcourt, Brace. First book printing of the sonnet "Grow not too high, grow not too far from home" on p. 117, with credit to *Harper's* (for September, 1925).

THE CONNING TOWER BOOK. Edited by F. P. A. Macy-Masius Publishers, New York. First book printing of "The Armistice Day Parade" on p. 219, by Nancy Boyd, which had appeared in *The New York World* for   1925. This has not been reprinted in book form elsewhere. Also,

Edna St. Vincent Millay

on p. 101, is a poem by Witter Bynner, "To Edna St. Vincent Millay."

THE BEST POEMS OF 1926. Selected by Thomas Moult and decorated by John Austen. New York, Harcourt, Brace. First book printing of "The Pioneer" (sonnet) on p. 12, with credit to *The Saturday Review of Literature* for December. This is error: the poem appeared in *Saturday Review* for August 29, 1925.

AMERICAN POETRY 1927: A MISCELLANY. New York, Harcourt, Brace & Company. Published August, 1927. First book printing of the sonnet "Not that it matters, not that my heart's cry" on p. 242, and of "Sonnet to Gath" on p. 243. Also contains the sonnet "Grow not too high, grow not too far from home."

AMERICA ARRAIGNED. Edited by Lucia Trent and Ralph Cheyney, with an introduction by John Haynes Holmes. New York, Dean & Co., 1928. Published January, 1928. First book printing of "Justice Denied in Massachusetts" on pp. 79-80.

ANTHOLOGY DE LA NOUVELLE POÉSIE AMÉRICAINE par Eugène Jolas. Edition originale, Kra, 6 Rue Blanche, Paris. The first edition of 100 copies, printed in 1928, is identified by the words Edition Originale. This contains "God's World", translated as "Le Monde de Dieu", and is the only translation into French of a Millay poem that I know of. See periodical list for 1918 and 1927 for Spanish and Yiddish translations.

OUTCROP. Poems by Abbé Huston Evans, with a foreword by Edna St. Vincent Millay. Harper & Brothers, New York, 1928. First edition (1,000 copies), so marked on verso of

Bibliography

title-page, printed in March, 1928; the first 25 copies were autographed by the author.

YIDDISH AMERICA: An Anthology. Edited by Noah Steinberg. New York, Verlag Leben, 1929. The contents of this book are in the Yiddish language. First book printing of translations into Yiddish by Dr. A. Asen of "I Shall Go Back Again to the Bleak Shore", "Spring", and "Lament", on pp. 209-210.

MOUNTAIN AGAINST MOUNTAIN, by Arthur Davison Ficke. New York, Doubleday, Doran, 1929. Blurb by Miss Millay on inside flap of dust jacket.

THE BOOK OF SONNET SEQUENCES. Edited by Houston Peterson. Longmans, Green and Co., New York, 1929. First book printing of the sonnet "I do but ask that you be always fair" and of the sonnet "I only know that every hour with you," included in the first (and only) book printing, on pp. 399-410, of the sequence, *Twenty Sonnets,* which first appeared in *Reedy's Mirror* in April and May, 1920.

UNBOUND ANTHOLOGY. Sometime in 1930 The Poets' Guild, Christodom House, New York, reprinted three poems, each separately in broadside form measuring 5 x 7½, with the poem on the obverse and a note of presentation to The Unbound Anthology on the reverse. These broadsides were issued in editions of about 300 copies, and constitute first separate printings of the poems "Song of a Second April", "The Little Ghost", and "God's World."

CHRISTMAS CARD. About 200 Christmas cards bearing an unpublished poem of four lines were printed in Lutetia type and sent by Miss Millay as a greeting in December of 1930.

Edna St. Vincent Millay

HARPER BOOKS SPRING 1931. Harper & Brothers' catalogue for the spring of 1931 carries an announcement of *Fatal Interview* on p. 18, and the sonnet "Moon, that against the lintel of the west" is printed in full.

THE GOURMETS ALMANAC, by Allan Ross Macdougall. London, Desmond Harmsworth, MCMXXXI. On p. v of this interesting book the name of Edna St. Vincent Millay tops the list of servers of good provender, and on p. xxv the compiler has made an "envoy" by adding a quatrain from an unpublished poem by "E. St. V. M." to a couplet of "R. L. S."

A DAY ON SKATES, the Story of a Dutch Picnic. By Hilda Van Stockum. Foreword by Edna St. Vincent Millay. New York, Harper & Brothers, 1934 (May). One page foreword.

MY HOUSE OF LIFE, an Autobiography. By Jessie B. Rittenhouse, with illustrations. Boston, Houghton Mifflin, 1934. On pp. 253-255 is a letter from Miss Millay to the author, dated April 7, 1920. On pp. 249-253 is a discussion of the appearance of "Renascence" in *The Lyric Year*, and facing p. 254 is a portrait of Miss Millay by Berenice Abbott.

MEMORY OF LOVE, by Bessie Breuer. New York, Simon and Schuster, 1935. There is a blurb by Miss Millay on the front and back of the dust jacket, a total of about ten lines.

b. POEMS SET TO MUSIC

THURSDAY, with music composed by Horace Johnson. Published August 6, 1923, by G. Schirmer, Inc., New York.

FROM A VERY LITTLE SPHINX (seven poems), with music

Bibliography

composed by Bernard Wagenaar. Published January 30, 1926, by G. Schirmer, Inc., New York.

THE KING'S HENCHMAN. See various collations *infra*.

MY CANDLE, with music composed by Annabel Morris Buchanan. Published January 4, 1928, by G. Ricordi & Co., Inc., New York.

THE RETURN FROM TOWN, with music composed by Constance Herreshoff. Published July 18, 1928, by J. Fischer & Bro., New York.

AFTERNOON ON A HILL, with music composed by Arthur Farwell, and HORSE SHOE, with music composed by Kenneth Smith, are on pp. 74 and 167 of *New Songs for New Voices*, Edited by Louis Untermeyer and Clara and David Mannes. New York, Harcourt, Brace & Co. (1928.)

THE LITTLE TAVERN, with music composed by Ruth Wright Vanderlip. Published June 18, 1929, by Oliver Ditson Co., Boston.

ELAINE, with music composed by Constance Mills Herreshoff. Published May 25, 1931, by J. Fischer & Bro., New York.

GOD'S WORLD, with music composed by Jacques Wolfe. Published July 6, 1932, by G. Schirmer, Inc., New York.

GOD'S WORLD, with music composed by William H. Schuman. Published May 11, 1933, by Marks Music Corp., New York.

WHERE SHE LIES, with music composed by Henry Cowell.

SECTION III

PERIODICALS

PERIODICALS

Note: *The Megunticook* was a Camden, Maine, high school journal. I have not seen any copies of it, and the list of Miss Millay's contributions to it came to me indirectly; only one of them, the last given below, have I been able to check, through the Camden Public Library
K. Y.

Forest Trees	*St. Nicholas*, October, 1906. 33: 1142.
The Land of Romance	*St. Nicholas*, March, 1907. 34: 464.
The Land of Romance	*Current Literature*, April, 1907. 42:456-7.
After the Celebration (as told by the fire-cracker)	*St. Nicholas*, July, 1907. 34:859.
Vacation Song	*St. Nicholas*, August, 1907. 34: 954.
Poet Laureate to the King	*The Megunticook*, 1907. ??
Ode to an Under-Classman	*The Megunticook*, anon? date ?
Ode to a Class-Mate	*The Megunticook*, date ?
Life	*St. Nicholas*, April, 1908. 35:571.
Day's Rest-time	*St. Nicholas*, November, 1908. 36:85.
As Others See Us	*The Megunticook*, December, 1908.
When the Cat's Away, a story	*The Megunticook*, December, 1908.
La Joie de Vivre (commencement oration	*The Megunticook*, June, 1909. 8:25.

in the form of a poem)	
Young Mother Hubbard	*St. Nicholas*, August, 1909. 36:952.
Friends	*St. Nicholas*, May, 1910. 37:660.
Letter to the editor of Farewell to the League	*St. Nicholas*, October, 1910. 37:1146.
Renascence	*Reedy's Mirror*, December 19, 1912.
Renascence	*Forum*, January, 1913. 49:102.
Excerpts (Renascence)	*Current Opinion*, February, 1913. 54:150.
Journey	*Forum*, May, 1913. 49:630.
Journey	*Current Opinion*, June, 1913. 54:497.
God's World	*Forum*, July, 1913. 50:1.
God's World	*Current Opinion*, September, 1913. 55:203.
Interim	*Vassar Miscellany Monthly*, July, 1914. 43:9:597-602.
Interim	*Forum*, September, 1914. 52:332-7.
The Shroud	*Forum*, October, 1914. 52:498.
Sorrow	*Forum*, November, 1914. 52:764.
Barbara on the Beach —prose	*Smart Set*, November, 1914. 44:3:26 ff.
Indifference	*Forum*, March, 1915. 53:334.
The Dream	*Forum*, July, 1915. 54:38.
Ashes of Life	*Forum*, August, 1915. 54:183.
Ashes of Life	*Current Opinion*, September, 1915. 59:200.

Bibliography

The Suicide	*Vassar Miscellany Monthly,* April, 1916. I:7:383-6.
If You Were Dead (If I should learn, in some quite casual way)	*Forum,* May, 1916. 55:497.
Blue Beard	*Forum,* May, 1916. 55:498.
Witch-wife	*Forum,* May, 1916. 55:498.
'17 Prize Song	*The Patient Periodical* (Vassar), May 12, 1916. 1:29:1-5.
Why Did I Ever Come to This Place?	*Vassar Miscellany Monthly,* December, 1916. II:2:85.
The Wall of Dominoes, a play	*Vassar Miscellany Monthly,* May, 1917. II:7:286-303.
Baccalaureate Hymn	*Vassar Quarterly,* July, 1917. 2:4:258.
Kin to Sorrow	*Poetry,* August, 1917. 10:234.
The Little Tavern	*Poetry,* August, 1917. 10:234-5.
Afternoon on a Hill	*Poetry,* August, 1917. 10:235.
Afternoon on a Hill	*Literary Digest,* September 8, 1917. 55:10:37.
The Little Tavern	*Literary Digest,* September 8, 1917. 55:10:37.
Sonnet (Time does not bring relief)	*Century,* December, 1917. 95:213.
Sonnet (Time does not bring relief)	*Current Opinion,* January, 1918. 64:1:58.
Sonnet (Time does not bring relief)	*Literary Digest,* March 9, 1918. 56:10:36.
God's World	*Reedy's Mirror,* March 29, 1918. 27:13:194.
When the year grows old	*Current Opinion,* April, 1918. 64:282.

Edna St. Vincent Millay

God's World	*Current Opinion*, April, 1918. 64:282.
Sonnet (Not in this chamber), with Spanish translation by J. Glenton	*Pan-American Monthly*, May, 1918. 27:40.
Figs from Thistles (First Fig, Second Fig, Unexplorer, Penitent, Thursday).	*Poetry*, June, 1918. 12:130-1.
Figs from Thistles	*Literary Digest*, June 29, 1918. 57:13:36-8.
The Penitant (sic)	*Reedy's Mirror*, June 7, 1918. 27:23:339.
Ashes of Life with Spanish translation by Pedro Henriquez Urena	*Pan-American Monthly*, July, 1918. 27:158.
The Shroud with Spanish translation by Christina Salavatierra	*Pan-American Monthly*, July, 1918. 27:159.
The Penitent	*Current Opinion*, August, 1918. 65:123-4.
Possession (I know I said, "I am weary of you—go!")	*The Sonnet*, October, 1918. 1:10:1.
Humoresque	*The Dial*, October 19, 1918. 65:293.
Elaine	*Nation*, November 16, 1918. 107:578.
Daphne	*Ainslee's*, November, 1918. 42:4:40.

Bibliography

Lord Archer, Death	*Ainslee's*, December, 1918. 42:5: 133.
Quanti dolci pensier, quanto disio (We talk of taxes and I call you friend)	*The Dial*, December 28, 1918. 65:601.
Fugitive	*Ainslee's*, January, 1919. 42:6:67.
Elaine	*Current Opinion*, January, 1919. 66:53.
A Visit to the Asylum	*Ainslee's*, February, 1919. 43:1: 91.
Rondel	*Ainslee's*, March, 1919. 43:2:145.
Love Resurgent	*Ainslee's*, April, 1919. 43:3:60.
She is Overheard Singing	*Poetry*, May, 1919. 14:67.
Recuerdo	*Poetry*, May, 1919. 14:68.
She is Overheard Singing	*Reedy's Mirror*, May 15, 1919, vol. p ?.
That which is Love's	*Ainslee's*, May, 1919. 43:4:69.
Young Love (Boyd)	*Ainslee's*, May, 1919. 43:4:70-80.
Unshriven	*Ainslee's*, June, 1919. 43:5:76.
Alms	*Ainslee's*, June, 1919. 43:5:144.
Low-tide	*Ainslee's*, July, 1919. 43:6:93.
The Door (Boyd)	*Ainslee's*, July, 1919. 43:6:130-140.
Departure	*Ainslee's*, August, 1919. 44:1:51.
The Dark Horse (Boyd)	*Ainslee's*, September, 1919. 44:2: 57-67.
Shrine	*Ainslee's*, September, 1919. 44:2: 90.
Departure	*Current Opinion*, September, 1919. 67:191.

Edna St. Vincent Millay

The Seventh Stair (Boyd)	*Ainslee's,* October, 1919. 44:3:1-56.
Rosemary	*Ainslee's,* October, 1919. 44:3:56.
The Death of Autumn	*The Nation,* October 25, 1919. 109:544.
Inland	*Ainslee's,* November, 1919. 44:4:57.
Innocents at Large (Boyd)	*Ainslee's,* December, 1919. 44:5:122-34.
Exiled	*Ainslee's,* December, 1919. 44:5:146.
The White Peacock (Boyd)	*Ainslee's,* January, 1920. 44:6:97-104.
Elegy Before Death	*Ainslee's,* January, 1920. 44:6:104.
Song of a Second April	*Ainslee's,* February, 1920. 45:1:61.
Death of Autumn	*Current Opinion,* February, 1920. 68:247.
To Love Impuissant (Love, though for this you riddle me with darts)	*The Dial,* March, 1920. 68:342.
Mirage (Once more into my arid days like dew)	*Ainslee's,* March, 1920. 45:2:116.
Aria da Capo	*Reedy's Mirror,* March 18, 1920. 29:12:199-202.
Sonnet (Oh, my beloved, have you thought of this)	*Ainslee's,* April, 1920. 45:3:119.
Elegy Before Death	*Current Opinion,* April, 1920. 68:545.

Bibliography

Doubt no more that Oberon   *The Nation,* April 13, 1920. 110: 431.

Twenty Sonnets   *Reedy's Mirror,* April 29, 1920. 29:18:348.

    I. I shall forget you presently, my dear
   II. Loving you less than life, a little less
  III. Into the golden vessel of great song
  IV. How healthily their feet upon the floor
   V. Love is not blind; I see with single eye

The Bean Stalk   *Poetry,* May, 1920. 16:74-5.

Mirage   *Current Opinion,* May, 1920. 68: 692.

Mariposa   *Ainslee's,* May, 1920. 45:4:67.

Twenty Sonnets   *Reedy's Mirror,* May 6, 1920. 29: 19:369.

   VI. Not with libations, but with shouts and laughter
  VII. The light comes back with Columbine; she brings
VIII. Oh, think not I am faithful to a vow
  IX. I do but ask that you be always fair
   X. I pray you if you love me, bear my joy

Twenty Sonnets   *Reedy's Mirror,* May 13, 1920. 29:20:389.

   XI. I think I should have loved you presently
  XII. When I too long have looked upon your face
 XIII. And you as well must die, beloved dust
 XIV. I only know that every hour with you
  XV. Still will I harvest beauty where it grows

Twenty Sonnets   *Reedy's Mirror,* May 20, 1920. 29:21:409.

Edna St. Vincent Millay

Spring	*The Chapbook*, July, 1920. 3: 13:11.
Souvenir	*Ainslee's*, June-July, 1920. 45:5: 40.
Dead Music—An Elegy	*Vanity Fair*, July, 1920. 14:5:45.
Oh, think not	*Current Opinion*, July, 1920. 69: 1:128.
A Prayer to Persephone	*Vanity Fair*, August, 1920. 14:6: 57.
To Kathleen	*Ainslee's*, August, 1920. 45:6:130.
To the not impossible him	*Vanity Fair*, September, 1920. 15:1:53.
Nothing in Common (Boyd)	*Ainslee's*, September, 1920. 46:1: 83-94.
To the not impossible him	*Current Opinion*, October, 1920. 69:556.
Scrub	*Vanity Fair*, October, 1920. 15:2: 61.
Mr. Dallas Larabee, Sinner (Boyd)	*Ainslee's*, October, 1920. 46:2:80.
Wild Swans	*Vanity Fair*, November, 1920. 15:3:49.
The Singin' Woman from the Wood's Edge	*Vanity Fair*, November, 1920. 15:3:49.
When you that at this moment are to me	*Vanity Fair*, November, 1920. 15:3:49.

Bibliography

Here is a wound that never will heal I know	*Vanity Fair*, November, 1920. 15:3:49.
Pity me not because the light of day	*Vanity Fair*, November, 1920. 15:3:49.
What lips my lips have kissed and where and why	*Vanity Fair*, November, 1920. 15:3:49.
Spring	*Vanity Fair*, November, 1920. 15:3:49.
Weeds	*Vanity Fair*, November, 1920. 15:3:49.
The Bean Stalk	*Literary Digest*, November 13, 1920. 67:7:40.
To the not impossible him	*Literary Digest*, December 18, 1920. 67:12:38.
Daphne	*Literary Digest*, December 18, 1920. 67:12:38.
She is Overheard Singing	*Literary Digest*, December 18, 1920. 67:12-38.
Prayer to Persephone	*Current Opinion*, December, 1920. 69:879.
Scrub	*Current Opinion*, December, 1920. 69:879.
Assault	*New Republic*, December 29, 1920. 25:141.
Wraith	*Vanity Fair*, January, 1921. 15:5:63.
Rolls and Salt (Boyd)	*Vanity Fair*, January, 1921. 15:5:51.
Portrait by a Neighbor	*The Chapbook*, January, 1921. No. 19:14.

Edna St. Vincent Millay

The Pear Tree	*The Chapbook,* January, 1921. No. 19:15.
The Curse	*The Chapbook,* January, 1921. No. 19:16.
The Bean Stalk	*Current Opinion,* January, 1921. 70:123-4.
Doubt no more that Oberon	*Living Age,* January 15, 1921. 308:186.
The Hungry Heart	*Vanity Fair,* February, 1921. 15:6:49.
Assault	*Current Opinion,* February, 1921. 70:267.
To a poet that died young	*New Republic,* February 9, 1921. 25:315.
To a poet that died young	*Literary Digest,* February 26, 1921. 68:9:34.
The Implacable Aphrodite (Boyd)	*Vanity Fair,* March, 1921. 16:1:29.
Lament	*The Century,* March, 1921. 101:622.
Passer Mortuus Est	*The Century,* March, 1921. 101:622.
Sonnet (I see so clearly now my similar years)	*The Century,* March, 1921. 101:622.
The Goose Girl	*Vanity Fair,* April, 1921. 16:2:48.
To a poet that died young	*Current Opinion,* April, 1921. 70:553.
Breakfast in Bed (Boyd)	*Vanity Fair,* May, 1921. 16:3:53.
First Fig	*Current Opinion,* May, 1921. 70:697.

Bibliography

Penitent	*Current Opinion*, May, 1921. 70:697.
Unexplorer	*Current Opinion*, May, 1921. 70:697.
The Same Boat (Boyd)	*Vanity Fair*, June, 1921. 16:4:33.
The Pear Tree	*Living Age*, June 25, 1921. 309:794.
The Hungry Heart	*Current Opinion*, July, 1921. 71:124.
Pepper, Mostly (Boyd)	*Ainslee's*, August, 1921.
The Greek Dance: A Chorus of Hate (Boyd)	*Vanity Fair*, August, 1921. 16:6:47.
City Trees	*Literary Digest*, August 6, 1921. 70:6:36.
Prayer to Persephone	*Literary Digest*, August 6, 1921. 70:6:36.
Travel	*Literary Digest*, August 6, 1921. 70:6:36.
Assault	*Literary Digest*, August 6, 1921. 70:6:36.
Sonnet (What's this of death, from you who never will die?)	*New Republic*, August 24, 1921. 27:357.
Powder, Rouge and Lipstick (Boyd)	*Vanity Fair*, September, 1921. 17:1:43.
Inland	*Current Opinion*, September, 1921. 71:371.
Lament	*Current Opinion*, September, 1921. 71:371.

Edna St. Vincent Millay

Sowing the Rue	*Current Opinion,* September, 1921. 71:371.
Travel	*Current Opinion,* September, 1921. 71:371.
Wild Swans	*Current Opinion,* September, 1921. 71:372.
The Pond	*Gargoyle* (Paris), September, 1921. 1:3:11.
Art and How to Fake It (Boyd)	*Vanity Fair,* October, 1921. 17:2:37.
Elegy Before Death	*Vanity Fair,* October, 1921. 17:2:49.
Passer Mortuus Est	*Vanity Fair,* October, 1921. 17:2:49.
Travel	*Vanity Fair,* October, 1921. 17:2:49.
Song of a Second April	*Vanity Fair,* October, 1921. 17:2:49.
Alms	*Vanity Fair,* October, ·1921. 17:2:49.
Exiled	*Vanity Fair,* October, 1921. 17:2:49.
Elaine	*Vanity Fair,* October, 1921. 17:2:49.
Burial	*Vanity Fair,* October, 1921. 17:2:49.
Sonnet (Cherish you then the hope I shall forget)	*Vanity Fair,* October, 1921. 17:2:49.
Sentimental Solon (Boyd)	*Metropolitan,* October, 1921. 54:15.
The Philosopher	*Ainslee's,* November, 1921. vol. , p.

Bibliography

Cordially Yours (Boyd)	*Vanity Fair*, November, 1921. 17:3:35.
The Philosopher	*Current Opinion*, December, 1921. 71:804.
For Winter, For Summer (Boyd)	*Vanity Fair*, December, 1921. 17:4:48.
Tea for the Muse (Boyd)	*Vanity Fair*, January, 1922. 17:5:52.
Review of Elinor Wylie's *Nets to Catch the Wind*	*New York Evening Post Literary Review*, January 28, 1922.
The Dragon-Fly	*Vanity Fair*, February, 1922. 17:6:15.
Here Comes the Bride (Boyd)	*Vanity Fair*, February, 1922. 17:6:52.
Ships and Sealing Wax (Boyd)	*Vanity Fair*, March, 1922. 18:1:40.
Exiled	*Vanity Fair*, March, 1922. 18:1:44.
Out of Reach of the Baby (Boyd)	*Vanity Fair*, April, 1922. 18:2:45.
Sonnet (Oh, oh, you will be sorry for that word)	*Vanity Fair*, April, 1922. 18:2:70.
How to be Happy Though Good (Boyd)	*Vanity Fair*, May, 1922. 18:3:57.
I Said to Beauty	*Vanity Fair*, May, 1922. 18:3:59.
Knock Wood (Boyd)	*Vanity Fair*, June, 1922. 18:4:57.
The Ballad of the Harpweaver	*Vanity Fair*, June, 1922. 18:4:58.

Edna St. Vincent Millay

The Ballad of the Harpweaver	*Literary Digest*, June 3, 1922. 73:10:42.
Sonnet (Oh, oh, you will be sorry for that word)	*Bookman*, June, 1922. 55:514.
The Barrel—prose	*Vanity Fair*, July, 1922. 18:5:35.
I Like Americans (Boyd)	*Vanity Fair*, August, 1922. 18:6:44.
I Said to Beauty	*Bookman*, August, 1922. 55:604.
No Bigger than a Man's Hand (Boyd)	*Vanity Fair*, September, 1922. 19:1:48.
Song for The Lamp and the Bell	*Yale Review* n.s., October, 1922. 12:56.
Autumn Chant	*Yale Review* n.s., October, 1922. 12:56-7.
Look Me Up (Boyd)	*Vanity Fair*, October, 1922. 19:2:44.
To the Liberty Bell	*Liberator*, October, 1922. 5:15.
Autumn Chant	*Literary Digest*, October 14, 1922. 75:2:42.
Diary of an American Art Student in Paris (Boyd)	*Vanity Fair*, November, 1922. 19:3:44.
The Wood Road	*Vanity Fair*, November, 1922. 19:3:69.
Nuit Blanche	*Vanity Fair*, November, 1922. 19:3:69.
I know I am but summer to your heart	*Vanity Fair*, November, 1922. 19:3:69.
Say what you will and scratch my heart to find	*Vanity Fair*, November, 1922. 19:3:69.

Bibliography

The Key—prose	*Vanity Fair*, December, 1922. 19:4:45.
Honor Bright (Boyd)	*Vanity Fair*, December, 1922. 19:4:65.
Drama for the Deaf—prose	*Vanity Fair*, January, 1923. 19:5:51.
"Two Souls with but a Single Thought" (Boyd)	*Vanity Fair*, January, 1923. 19:5:63.
Memory of Cape Cod	*Rhythmus*, February, 1925. 1:2:25.
The Woman Who Would Be Moving the Beds About—prose	*Vanity Fair*, February, 1923. 19:6:35.
"Madame a Tort" (Boyd)	*Vanity Fair*, February, 1923. 19:6:46.
The Murder in The Fishing Cat—prose	*Century*, March, 1923. 105:663-75.
The Platter—prose	*Vanity Fair*, March, 1923. 20:1:65.
Our All American Almanac & Prophetic Messenger (Boyd)	*Vanity Fair*, March, 1923. 20:1:40.
Letter re play *Roger Bloomer*	*New York Times*, April 1, 1923, p. 8.
The Cairn	*Harpers*, April, 1923. 146:576.
Never May the Fruit Be Plucked	*Harpers*, April, 1923. 146:576.
Never May the Fruit Be Plucked	*The Chapbook*, April, 1923. 36:16.

[173]

Edna St. Vincent Millay

"Say Shibboleth"— *Vanity Fair*, April, 1923. 20:2:40.
prose

Sonnets from an Un- *Harpers*, May, 1923. 146:763-8.
grafted Tree

So she came back
The last white sawdust
She filled her arms
The white bark writhed
A wagon stopped before
Then cautiously she pushed
One way there was
She let them leave
Not over kind nor over quick
She had forgotten
It came into her mind
Tenderly, in those times
From the wan dream
She had a horror
There was upon the sill
The doctor asked her
Gazing upon him now

The Cairn   *Poetry*, May, 1923. 22:72-3.
The Concert   *Poetry*, May, 1923. 22:72-3.
The Concert   *Literary Digest*, May 19, 1923.
                   77:7:36.
To a Dying Man   *Vanity Fair*, June, 1923. 20:4:40.
To a Dying Man   *Current Opinion*, June, 1923.
                   74:736.
Never May the Fruit *Literary Digest*, June 9, 1923.
Be Plucked   77:10:36.
Renascence   *Literary Digest*, June 9, 1923.
                   77:10:36.

Bibliography

To a Dying Man	*Literary Digest*, June 9, 1923. 77:10:36.
Spring Song	*Literary Review*, June 16, 1923. 3:767.
The Concert	*Current Opinion*, July, 1923. 75:94-5.
The Cairn	*Current Opinion*, July, 1923. 75:94-5.
Keen	*Century*, July, 1923. 106:364.
Keen	*Literary Digest*, July 7, 1923. 78:1:42.
To a Dying Man	*Bookman*, August, 1923. 57:625.
Keen	*Current Opinion*, September, 1923. 75:351.
From a Very Little Sphinx (seven poems)	*Harpers*, October, 1923. 147:670-1.
Excerpts (from "Sphinx") — four poems 1, 5, 6, and 7.	*Literary Digest*, October 13, 1923. 79:2:38.
Portrait of a Neighbor	*Independent*, November 10, 1923. 111:216.
Sonnet (Oh, think not)	*Independent*, November 10, 1923. 111:216.
Unexplorer	*Current Opinion*, January, 1924. 76:95.
Recuerdo	*Current Opinion*, January, 1924. 76:95.
First Fig	*Current Opinion*, January, 1924. 76:95.
The Curse	*Vanity Fair*, January, 1924. 21:5:?

[175]

Edna St. Vincent Millay

The Curse	*Literary Digest,* January 26, 1924. 80:4:36.
The Curse	*Current Opinion,* February, 1924. 76:224.
Spring Song	*Current Opinion,* March, 1924. 76:350.
Feast	*Current Opinion,* March, 1924. 76:351.
Scrub	*Current Opinion,* March, 1924. 76:351.
The Poet and His Book	*The Dial,* January, 1925. 78:69.
Souvenir	*Golden Book,* June, 1925. 1:780.
The Pioneer	*Saturday Review of Literature,* August 29, 1925. 2:77.
Two Sonnets	*Harpers,* September, 1925. 151:439.

Not that it matters, not that my heart's cry
Grow not too high, grow not too far from home.

Not that it matters, not that my heart's cry	*Literary Digest,* September 5, 1925. 86:10:36.
Sonnet to Gath	*Vanity Fair,* September, 1925. 25:1:64.
Armistice Day Parade	*New York World,* ? 1925.
Armistice Day Parade	*Literary Digest,* December 19, 1925. 87:12:35.
Journey	*Golden Book,* January, 1926. 3:82.
The Pioneer	*Literary Digest,* January 16, 1926. 88:3:34.

Bibliography

The Concert — *Musical Quarterly,* January, 1927. 13:45-6.

All Hallows Eve (King's Henchman excerpt) — *Saturday Review of Literature,* February 19, 1927. 3:589-90.

Oh Caesar great wert thou (King's Henchman excerpt) — *Literary Digest,* March 19, 1927. 92:12:36.

Justice Denied in Massachusetts, — *New York World,* August 22, 1927, p. 2.

Letter (re Sacco-Vanzetti) — *New York World,* October 6, 1927, p. 12.

What Lips My Lips Have Kissed translated into Yiddish by A. Greenberg — *Der Oifkum,* October, 1927, 2:10:37.

When you that at this moment are to me translated into Yiddish by A. Greenberg — *Der Oifkum,* October, 1927. 2:10:37.

I shall go back again to the bleak shore translated into Yiddish by Dr. A. Asen — *Der Oifkum,* October, 1927. 2:10:37.

Spring translated into Yiddish by Dr. A. Asen — *Der Oifkum,* October, 1927. 2:10:38.

Lament translated into Yiddish by Dr. A. Asen — *Der Oifkum,* October, 1927. 2:10:38.

Fear — *Outlook,* November 9, 1927. 147:292-5.

[177]

Edna St. Vincent Millay

To Jesus on His Birthday	*McCall's,* December, 1927. 55:?:6.
To the wife of a sick friend	*Delineator,* March, 1928. 112:3:25.
The Bobolink	*Delineator,* May, 1928. 112:5:15.
On hearing a symphony	*New Republic,* June 13, 1928. 55:93.
Mist in the Valley	*Saturday Evening Post,* June 16, 1928. 200:51:5.
Song	*Saturday Evening Post,* June 16, 1928. 200:51:5.
The Buck in the Snow	*Saturday Evening Post,* June 16, 1928. 200:51:5.
Dirge Without Music	*Harpers,* July, 1928. 157:245.
Dirge Without Music	*Literary Digest,* July 7, 1928. 98:32.
I will give you the summer	*Saturday Evening Post,* August 4, 1928. 201:5:35.
Sonnet (Life, were thy pains as are the pains of hell)	*Saturday Evening Post,* August 4, 1928. 201:5:35.
Life	*Saturday Evening Post,* August 4, 1928. 201:5:35.
On first having heard the skylark	*Saturday Evening Post,* August 4, 1928. 201:5:35.
The Cameo	*New Republic,* August 22, 1928. 56:11.
When Caesar fell	*New Republic,* August 29, 1928. 56:45.
There at Dusk I Found You	*Delineator,* September, 1928. 113:3:14.

Bibliography

To a musician	*New Republic,* September 5, 1928. 56:72.
Lethe	*New Republic,* September 12, 1928. 56:98.
Dawn	*Saturday Evening Post,* September 15, 1928. 201:11:28.
To a young girl	*Saturday Evening Post,* September 15, 1928. 201:11:28.
Northern April	*Saturday Evening Post,* September 15, 1928. 201:11:28.
Portrait	*Saturday Review of Literature,* September 15, 1928. 5:117.
The Road to Avrillé	*Vanity Fair,* September, 1928. 31:1:62.
Lethe	*Literary Digest,* October 13, 1928. 99:2:46.
Moriturus	*Literary Digest,* October 27, 1928. 99:4:36.
To a musician	*Literary Digest,* October 27, 1928. 99:4:36.
Epitaph for the Race of Man	*St. Louis Post-Dispatch,* December 9, 1928. 81:94:Drift of Civilization section, p. 1.

Before this cooling planet shall be cold,—
His heatless room the watcher of the stars
The broken dike, the levee washed away,
He woke in terror to a sky more bright
Sweeter was loss than silver coins to spend,
Him not the golden fang of furious heaven,
Now sets his foot upon the eastern sill
Alas for Man, so stealthily betrayed,

Edna St. Vincent Millay

Only the diamond and the diamond's dust
Here lies, and none to mourn him but the sea,

The Buck in the Snow	*St. Nicholas,* March, 1929 56:346, 411.
Bobolink	*St. Nicholas,* March, 1929. 56:346, 411.
For Pao-chin	*St. Nicholas,* March, 1929. 56:346, 411.
Through the Green Forest	*Ladies' Home Journal,* March, 1930. 47:6.
Two sonnets in memory	*New Republic,* August 27, 1930. 64:34.

As men have loved their lovers in times past
Where can the heart be hidden in the ground

As men have loved	*Literary Digest,* September 20, 1930. 106:12:31.
Three sonnets:	*Poetry,* October, 1930. 37:1-3.

Women have loved before as I love now
I know my mind and I have made my choice
Even in the moment of our earliest kiss

Sonnets	*Harpers,* December, 1930. 162:1-3.

Moon, that against the lintel of the west
This beast that rends me in the sight of all
Time, that is pleased to lengthen out the day
Now by the path I climbed I journey back
If in the years to come you should recall

Being out of love	*Saturday Evening Post,* December 6, 1930. 203:23:9.
Strange thing	*Saturday Evening Post,* December 6, 1930. 203:23:9.

Bibliography

I dreamed I moved	*Saturday Evening Post*, December 6, 1930. 203:23:9.
Not in a silver	*Saturday Evening Post*, December 6, 1930. 203:23:9.
When you are dead	*Saturday Evening Post*, December 6, 1930. 203:23:9.
When we that wore	*Harpers*, January, 1931. 162:150.
There is a well	*Delineator*, January, 1931. 118:1:14.
If in the years	*Literary Digest*, January 10, 1931. 108:2:38.
Since of no creature	*Delineator*, February, 1931. 118:2:16.
My worship from this	*New Republic*, March 18, 1931. 66:117.
Sweet love, sweet thorn	*New Republic*, March 18, 1931. 66:117.
Shall I be prisoner	*New Republic*, March 18, 1931. 66:117.
Now by this moon	*New Republic*, March 18, 1931. 66:117.
When we are old	*New Republic*, March 25, 1931. 66:144.
Hearing your words	*New Republic*, March 25, 1931. 66:144.
Believe, if ever	*New Republic*, March 25, 1931. 66:144.
Oh, sleep forever	*New Republic*, March 25, 1931. 66:144.
Love me no more	*Harpers*, April, 1931. 162:548.
The heart once broken	*Harpers*, April, 1931. 162:548.

Edna St. Vincent Millay

Horseshoe	*National Educ. Assn. Journ.*, May, 1931. 20:185.
Hearing your words	*Literary Digest*, July 18, 1931. 110:3:29.
What lips my lips	*Golden Book*, August, 1931. 14:75.
Forest Trees	*St. Nicholas*, October, 1931. 58:cover.
November	*Library Journal*, November 15, 1932. 57:940.
Love Sonnet (When did I ever deny)	*Delineator*, August, 1933. 123:2:7.
Not so far as the forest	*Woman's Home Companion*, November, 1933. 60:?:9.
Above these cares	*Harpers*, December, 1933. 168:68.
Apostrophe to Man	*New York Herald Tribune Magazine*, December 17, 1933, p. 2.
Valentine	*Harpers*, February, 1934. 168:352.
Short Story	*Saturday Evening Post*, February 24, 1934. 206:35:23.
On thought in harness	*Saturday Evening Post*, February 24, 1934. 206:35:23.
Oak Leaves	*Saturday Evening Post*, February 24, 1934. 206:35:23.
If still your orchards bear	*Saturday Evening Post*, February 24, 1934. 206:35:23.
Wind	*Saturday Evening Post*, February 24, 1934. 206:35:23.
Epitaph	*New York Herald Tribune Magazine*, February 25, 1934, p. 12.

Bibliography

To a young poet	*New York Herald Tribune Magazine*, February 25, 1934, p. 12.
Aubade	*New York Herald Tribune Magazine*, February 25, 1934, p. 12.
From a train window	*Delineator*, October, 1934. 125:4:21.
Fawn	*Delineator*, October, 1934. 125:4:21.
If still your orchards bear	*Scholastic*, February 2, 1935. 26:12.
Sonnet: Now forth to meadow as the farmer goes	*Scholastic*, February 2, 1935. 26:12.
Conversation at Midnight	*Harpers*, November, 1935. 171:641-7.

One page explanation of poem sequence by Miss Millay

XVI. Anselmo said, and took in his brown hands
XVII. After a solemn pause, Anselmo said,
XVIII. "I want to talk," said Lucas, "about love!"
XXI. "Why, you never were alone in your life!
XXII. "This girl," said Lucas "—none of you know her name,
XXIII. "Lucas, Romantic Love is on the rocks,
XXIV. "That's not the point," Carl said; "the point is not
XXVII. "Not that the world is so much with us," Merton
XXVIII. "Yes, pack your bags—I beg your pardon, let
XXIX. "Your masses," Merton said, "Yes, yes, I know
XXX. "It's true I honor the dirt; that's perfectly true,"
XXXI. Over the sound of flushing water, which

Edna St. Vincent Millay

I too beneath your   *Delineator,*   August,   1936.
moon, almighty sex   129:2:3.

SECTION IV

CRITICISM

a. CRITICISM IN BOOKS

The New Era in American Poetry, by Louis Untermeyer. Holt, New York, 1919. Pp. 271-275 on Millay.

Flames of Faith, by William L. Stidger. The Abingdon Press, New York, 1922. Chapter on Edna Saint (*sic*) Vincent Millay, pp. 47-55.

Heavens, by Louis Untermeyer. New York, Harcourt, Brace, (1922). On p. 135 is "Empty Spaces" by Ed-a St. Vinc-nt Mill-y, a parody of twelve lines by Untermeyer.

A Tree With a Bird in It, by Margaret Widdemer. New York, Harcourt, Brace, 1922. On p. 46 is "Tea O' Herbs," a parody, and on p. 47 is a pen-and-ink sketch.

Sonnets of a Portrait Painter, by Arthur Davison Ficke. New York, 1922. The fifth section of the book is entitled "Epitaph for the Poet V. A Hymn to Intellectual Beauty. To Edna St. Vincent Millay."

American Poetry Since 1900, by Louis Untermeyer. New York, Harcourt, Brace, 1923. Pp. 214-221 contain biographical sketch, criticism, and portrait.

Our Best Poets English and American, by Theodore Maynard. London, 1924. Contains criticism, pp. 226 ff.

Many Minds, by Carl Van Doren. New York, Alfred A. Knopf, 1924. On pp. 105-120 is the article "Youth and Wings" that appeared in *Century Magazine* for June, 1923.

From Whitman to Sandburg in American Poetry, by Bruce Weirick. New York, Macmillan, 1924. Criticism on pp. 171-174.

Edna St. Vincent Millay

Taking a Literary Pulse, by Joseph Collins. Doran, New York, 1924. In chapter six, on pp. 118-120, Miss Millay is considered under "Gallantry and Our Women Writers."

Chaucer's Nuns and Other Essays, by Sister M. Madeleva. Appleton, New York, 1925. Pp. 143-158 concern Miss Millay under the title, "Where are you going, my pretty maid?"

Poets of America, by Clement Wood. Dutton, New York, (1925). Chapter twelve is entitled "Edna St. Vincent Millay: A Clever Sappho." Pp. 199-213.

Poets and Their Art, by Harriet Monroe. Macmillan, New York, 1926. Contains "Edna St. Vincent Millay" on pp. 63-71, a reprint of the article that appeared in *Poetry* magazine for August, 1924.

Edna St. Vincent Millay, in The Pamphlet Poets series. Simon & Schuster, New York, (1927). A four-page introduction by Hughes Mearns precedes Miss Millay's own selection of thirteen poems, none of which is a first printing, the object being merely to present a representative group.

Minor Prophecies, by Lee Simonson. New York, Harcourt, Brace, (1927). "Minority Report" on pp. 119-137 is an attack on "The King's Henchman" as an opera because of the alleged plethora of sibilants.

Edna St. Vincent Millay. Youth and Wings, Edna St. Vincent Millay: Singer, by Carl Van Doren (ca. 1927). Reprinted from *Many Minds,* separately.

Poems in Praise of Practically Nothing, by Samuel Hoffenstein. Boni & Liveright, New York, (1928). On p. 143

Bibliography

is "Miss Millay Says Something Too," a parody of the poem "Exiled," and on p. 144 is a parody of "The Goose Girl."

Ten Modern Poets, by Rica Brenner. Harcourt, New York, (1930). On pp. 63-81 is a chapter devoted to Miss Millay and a portrait faces p. 80.

The Provincetown, a Story of the Theatre, by Helen Deutsch and Stella Hanan. New York, (1931). Portrait on p. 32.

The Little World, 1914 and After, by Alfred Kreymborg. New York, Coward-McCann, (1932). On p. 150 is a lampoon.

Selected Poems of Robert Nathan. Alfred A. Knopf, New York, 1935. On p. 3 is a sonnet "For Edna St. Vincent Millay."

Reactionary Essays on Poetry and Ideas, by Allen Tate. Scribners, New York, 1936. On pp. 221-228 is an essay on Miss Millay, which is the same review of *Fatal Interview* that appeared in the *New Republic* for May 6, 1931.

Edna St. Vincent Millay and Her Times, by Elizabeth Atkins. Chicago. The University of Chicago Press, 1936. This 284-page book traces the widespread changes in American poetry, and shows the relationship of Miss Millay to these changes from 1912 onward. It includes critical evaluations of all Miss Millay's books.

Edna St. Vincent Millay

b. CRITICISM IN PERIODICALS

A Poet of Renascence, by William S. Braithwaite. *Boston Transcript,* February 6, 1918.

Review of *Second April,* by Maxwell Anderson. *The Measure,* September, 1921.

Miss Millay's Poems, by Padraic Colum. *The Freeman,* November 2, 1921. 4:189.

Review of *Second April,* by O. W. Firkins. *Independent,* November 19, 1921. 107:194.

An American Poetess. *Times Literary Supplement,* London, March 30, 1922.

Article in *The Bookman,* November, 1922. 56:272-8.

Hall of Fame. *Vanity Fair,* April, 1923. 20:4:72.

Youth and Wings. Edna St. Vincent Millay, Singer, by Carl Van Doren. *Century,* June, 1923. 106:310-16.

Her Massive Sandal, by Genevieve Taggard. *The Measure,* April, 1924.

Edna St. Vincent Millay, by Harriet Monroe. *Poetry,* August, 1924. 24:260-6.

Edna St. Vincent Millay, by Witter Bynner. *New Republic,* December 10, 1924. 41:14-15.

Article by Genevieve Taggard. *Equal Rights,* March 14, 1925.

A Nightingale at the Court of King Eadgar, by Elinor Wylie. *New York Herald Tribune,* February 20, 1927.

The King's Henchman, criticism. *Outlook,* March 2, 1927. 145:268-70.

Bibliography

The King's Henchman, criticism. *Nation,* March 9, 1927. 124:263.

The King's Henchman, criticism. *New Republic,* March 16, 1927. 50:101.

A Triumph for American Opera. *Literary Digest,* March 19, 1927. 92:12:27-28.

Miss Millay Goes Over the Top; The King's Henchman, by C. W. Ferguson. *The Bookman,* March, 1927. 65:83-5.

Woman of the Hour. *Woman Citizen,* April, 1927. 11 n.s.:7.

Edna St. Vincent Millay, by John Hyde Preston. *Virginia Quarterly,* July, 1927.

Edna St. Vincent Millay, by J. Grobard (in Yiddish) *Der Oifkum,* October, 1927. 2:10:35-6.

Edna St. Vincent Millay, by Edward Davison. *The English Journal,* November, 1927, pp. 671-682.

Miss Millay's New Volume of Poetry, by Henry W. Lanier. *St. Nicholas,* March, 1929. 56:346.

Edna St. Vincent Millay, by Ed. Windfield Parks. *Sewanee Review,* January, 1930.

Edna Millay's Fine Sonnets on First Love, by Percy Hutchinson. *New York Times Book Review,* April 19, 1931.

A Woman's Anatomy of Love, by Genevieve Taggard. *New York Herald Tribune Books,* April 19, 1931.

The Reascending Sonnet, by O. W. Firkins. *Saturday Review of Literature,* May 2, 1931.

Miss Millay's Sonnets, by A. Tate. *New Republic,* May 6, 1931. 66:335-6.

Edna St. Vincent Millay

Advance or Retreat? by Harriet Monroe. *Poetry*, July, 1931. 38:216-21

Rolfius and Miss Millay, by A. K. Smole. *New Republic,* July 15, 1931. 67:237.

New Writers, by E. McInnis. *Canadian Forum*, August, 1931. 11:424-5.

Edna St. Vincent Millay, by Naomi Royde-Smith. *Time and Tide,* London, October 17, 1931.

Intimate Glimpses of a Famous Poet, by Elizabeth Breuer. *Pictorial Review*, November, 1931. 33:2.

Best Sellers in Verse, by Jerome Beatty. *American Magazine*, January, 1932. 113:1:36-7 ff.

Poem "To Edna St. Vincent Millay." *St. Nicholas*, October, 1931.

Edna St. Vincent Millay. *Mercure de France,* Paris, November 1, 1931.

Edna St. Vincent Millay. *St. Nicholas*, November, 1931. Inside cover.

Review of *Fatal Interview*, by Louis Bonnerot. *Revue Anglo-Américaine,* Paris, December, 1932.

Edna Millay Finds a Cook, by Floyd Dell. *New York Herald Tribune Magazine*, March 19, 1933.

Une Poetesse Anglaise, by André Fontainas. *Figaro*, Paris, May 13, 1933.

Edna St. Vincent Millay, by Lawrence A. Conrad. *Landmark*, June, 1933.

Husband of a Genius; interview with E. J. Boissevain, by

Bibliography

A. R. Macdougall. *Delineator*, October, 1934. 125:21 et seq.

Review of *Wine From These Grapes*. *New York Times Book Review*, November 4, 1934.

Review of *Wine From These Grapes*. *Time*, November 5, 1934, p. 69.

Round about Parnassus, by William Rose Benet. *Saturday Review of Literature*, November 10, 1934. 11:279.

Review of *Wine From These Grapes*. *New York Herald Tribune Books*, November 11, 1934.

Edna Millay's Maturity, by P. B. Rice. *Nation*, November 14, 1934. 139:568 et seq.

Answer to Millay. Two sonnets by Robert Nathan. *Harpers*, February, 1935. 170:311.

Conversion into self, by L. Bogan. *Poetry*, February, 1935. 45:277-9.

Poetry Corner, by D. Emerson. *Scholastic*, February 2, 1935. 26:12.

Parody, by Louis Untermeyer. *New Yorker*, May 18, 1935, p. 18.

Review of *Flowers of Evil*. *Saturday Review of Literature*, April 4, 1936. 13:23:15.

Edna St. Vincent Millay's Youth, by Ethel Knight Fisher. *St. Nicholas*, September, 1936. 63:11:48; continued in October, 1936, issue. 63:12:52.

Edna St. Vincent Millay

c. PORTRAITS

Vanity Fair (of "Nancy Boyd")	November, 1921.	17:3:25.
Bookman	November, 1922.	56:272.
Century	June, 1923.	106:310.
Outlook	June 6, 1923.	134:113.
Literary Digest	June 9, 1923.	77:10:30.
Current Opinion	July, 1923.	75:50.
Literary Review	October 4, 1924.	5:4.
Collier's	March 14, 1925.	75:17.
Collier's	January 8, 1927.	79:11.
Collier's	September 3, 1927.	80:21.
Saturday Review of Literature	February 19, 1927.	3:589.
Outlook	March 2, 1927.	145:268.
Literary Digest	March 19, 1927.	92:12:27.
Woman Citizen	April, 1927.	11 ns.:7.
Review of Reviews	April, 1927.	75:435.
Outlook	November 9, 1927.	147:292.
Woman's Home Companion	November, 1927.	54:22.
Ladies' Home Journal	March, 1928.	45:22.
Delineator	September, 1928.	113:14.
World's Work	October, 1928.	56:654.
Bookman	January, 1930.	70:535.
Good Housekeeping	December, 1930.	91:82.
Wilson Bulletin	February, 1931.	5:381.
Saturday Review of Literature	May 2, 1931.	7:793.
Arts & Decoration	June, 1931.	35:56.
Pictorial Review	November, 1931.	33:2.
American Magazine	January, 1932.	113:36.
Bookman	December, 1932.	75:779.
Delineator	August, 1933.	123:7.
Literary Digest	February 3, 1934.	117:5:41.

Bibliography

Delineator	October, 1934.	125:4:21.
News-Week	November 3, 1934.	4:40.
Scholastic	February 2, 1935.	26:12.
Saturday Review of Literature	April 4, 1936.	13:23:15.

SECTION V

INDEX

NOTE TO THE INDEX

THIS is an index to the bibliography only, and not to the pages of the essay. Unfortunately, Mr. Cook and I worked separately, and I compiled the index, which is to be taken in conjunction with the other sections of the bibliography, while I was working on the other sections.

This index provides directional service to pages, but more importantly gives alphabetically segregated check lists of material that appears in the collations (especially the tables of contents), and in the periodical, appearance, and criticism lists. Each poem is traced through all its printings in the books and periodicals mentioned in Sections I to IV.

Books which are collated in Section I of the bibliography are set in capitals and small capitals; all other books, containing either appearances or criticism, and music, are set in small capitals. Periodicals, both magazines and newspapers, are set in italic, upper and lower case, and all other entries not classified in the three groups just mentioned, are set in roman upper and lower case. Poem and prose titles, proper names, and subject titles appear in the last group.

Articles are subordinated to the next succeeding word, in all languages, except in sonnet first lines, where of course the article is essential to the metre and may not be displaced.

Sonnets have been placed in a separate section, directly following the letter "S", in addition to their scattered ap-

Index

pearance. In this special sonnet section the first line to the sonnet is the key card, and a card of reference in that section refers to another card in that section only. In the general section the title to a sonnet, if such there be, is the key card, otherwise the first line is again the key card. Cards of reference in the general section refer to other cards in the general section. A poem which has been printed under more than one title will be found by reference under the title used in the collated book in which it was first printed.

To the best of my knowledge, Miss Millay published no poems under the name of Nancy Boyd, although she did publish prose items under her own name as well as the pseudonym. Therefore I have merely put the word "prose" to all prose articles issued under the name of Millay, and unless the name Boyd is specified, it is understood that all poems and prose items are by Millay.

Deriving, as it does, from them, the index is no more complete than the other sections of the bibliography: the material is presented in alphabetical rather than chronological fashion. I have in mind in making this statement the fact that the list of critical articles in periodicals (Section IVb) can and will be augmented by casual searching. For me to attempt a complete list would require more time and money than the subject warrants.

K. Y.

Index

· Index

Index

Index

Index

Index

Index

Index

Index

Index

Grow not too high, grow not too far from home (sonnet) —*Harpers*, September, 1925; BEST POEMS OF 1925; AMERICAN POETRY 1927 A MISCELLANY; THE BUCK IN THE SNOW.

Grown-up—A FEW FIGS FROM THISTLES, 1921; same, 1922; same, 1923; POEMS; POEMS SELECTED FOR YOUNG PEOPLE.

H

Haddon Craftsmen, p. 133.

Hall of Fame, p. 190.

Hamilton, Hamish, pp. 132, 133, 141, 143.

Hanan, Stella, p. 189.

Hangman's Oak—THE BUCK IN THE SNOW.

Harbor Press, The, p. 141.

Harcourt, Brace and Company, Inc., pp. 150, 151, 152, 155, 187, 188.

Hardy Garden, The—THE BUCK IN THE SNOW.

Harmsworth, Desmond, p. 154.

Harper & Brothers, pp. 96, 97, 99, 103, 106, 107, 108, 109, 112, 113, 114, 119, 122, 123, 127, 128, 132, 133, 135, 136, 139, 142, 152, 154.

HARPER BOOKS, SPRING 1931 (appearance), p. 154.

Harpers (Magazine)

1923

April: The Cairn, Never May the Fruit Be Plucked

May: Sonnets from an Ungrafted Tree

October: From a Very Little Sphinx

1925

September: Not that it matters, not that my heart's cry, Grow not too high, grow not too far from home

1928

July: Dirge Without Music

Harpers (Magazine) — (Continued)

1930

December: Moon that against the lintel of the west, This beast that rends me in the sight of all, Time that is pleased to lengthen out the day, Now by the path I climbed I journey back, If in the years to come you should recall

1931

January: When we that wore the myrtle wear the dust

April: Love me no more now let the god depart, The heart once broken is a heart no more

1933

December: Above these cares

1934

February: Valentine

1935

February: Answer to Millay by Robert Nathan

November: Conversation at Midnight

HARP-WEAVER AND OTHER POEMS, THE (book) —See coll. 19, p. 99, coll. 23, p. 104.

Hawkweed, The—THE BUCK IN THE SNOW.

Hearing your words, and not a word among them (sonnet) — *New Republic*, March 25, 1931; FATAL INTERVIEW; *Literary Digest*, July 18, 1931.

Heart, have no pity on this house of bone (sonnet) —FATAL INTERVIEW.

Heartman, Charles F., p. 76.

HEAVENS (criticism), p. 187.

Hedge of Hemlocks, The—WINE FROM THESE GRAPES.

He heard the coughing tiger in the night (sonnet) —WINE FROM THESE GRAPES.

Henderson, Alice Corbin, p. 147.

Index

Index

Index

In the Rotary Club and in the Communistic State—*Harpers*, November, 1935; CONVERSATION AT MIDNIGHT.

Intimate Glimpses of a Famous Poet, p. 192.

Into the golden vessel of great song (sonnet) —*Reedy's Mirror*, April 29, 1920; SECOND APRIL; POEMS; BOOK OF SONNET SEQUENCES.

It came into her mind, seeing how the snow (sonnet) —*Harpers*, May, 1923; THE HARP-WEAVER AND OTHER POEMS.

"It's true I honor the dirt; that's perfectly true,"—*Harpers*, November, 1935; CONVERSATION AT MIDNIGHT.

J

Joie de Vivre, La—*The Megunticook*, June, 1909.

Jolas, Eugene, p. 152.

Johnson, Horace, p. 154.

Journey—*The Forum*, May, 1913; *Current Opinion*, June, 1913; SECOND APRIL; POEMS; *Golden Book*, January, 1926; POEMS SELECTED FOR YOUNG PEOPLE.

Justice Denied in Massachusetts—*New York World*, August 22, 1927; AMERICA ARRAIGNED; THE BUCK IN THE SNOW.

K

Keen—*Century*, July, 1923; *Literary Digest*, July 7, 1923; *Current Opinion*, September, 1923; THE HARP-WEAVER AND OTHER POEMS.

Keller, Elizabeth, p. 150.

Kelmscott Chaucer, p. 104.

Kennerley, Mitchell, pp. 75, 79, 88, 91, 104, 108, 109, 150.

Key, The—prose—*Vanity Fair*, December, 1922.

Kidd, John G., p. 98.

KING'S HENCHMAN, THE (book) — coll. 29, p. 110; coll. 30, p. 111; coll. 30A, p. 112; coll. 31, p. 113; coll. 32, p. 114; coll. 33, p. 115; coll. 34, p. 116; excerpt p. 177; criticism pp. 188, 190, 191.

Kin to Sorrow—*Poetry*, August, 1917; RENASCENCE AND OTHER POEMS; POEMS.

Knock Wood—Boyd—*Vanity Fair*, June, 1922; DISTRESSING DIALOGUES.

Knopf, Alfred A., pp. 187, 189.

Kreymborg, Alfred, p. 189.

L

Ladies Home Journal
March, 1928: portrait
March, 1930: Through the Green Forest

Lament—*Century*, March, 1921; SECOND APRIL; *Current Opinion*, September, 1921; POEMS; *Der Oifkum*, October, 1927; YIDDISH AMERICA: AN ANTHOLOGY (trans.); POEMS SELECTED FOR YOUNG PEOPLE.

LAMP AND THE BELL, THE (book) — coll. 8, p. 86; coll. 12, p. 91; coll. 16, p. 96; coll. 24, p. 105.

Landmark, June, 1933, article by Lawrence A. Conrad.

Land of Romance, The—*St. Nicholas*, March, 1907; *Current Literature*, April, 1907.

Lankes, J. J., p. 151.

Lanier, Henry W., p. 191.

Leaf and the Tree, The—WINE FROM THESE GRAPES.

Lethe—*New Republic*, September 12, 1928; THE BUCK IN THE SNOW; *Literary Digest*, October 13, 1928.

Letters—*St. Nicholas*, October, 1910; *New York Times*, April 1, 1923; *New York World*, October 6, 1927; MY HOUSE OF LIFE.

Index

Let you not say of me when I am old (sonnet) —SECOND APRIL; POEMS.

Liberator, October, 1922: To the Liberty Bell.

Library Journal, November 15, 1932: November.

Life—*St. Nicholas*, April, 1908; *Saturday Evening Post*, August 4, 1928.

Life, were thy pains as are the pains of hell (sonnet) —*Saturday Evening Post*, August 4, 1928; THE BUCK IN THE SNOW.

Lines for a Grave-Stone—WINE FROM THESE GRAPES.

Literary Digest

1917
September 8: Afternoon on a Hill, The Little Tavern

1918
March 9: Time does not bring relief; you all have lied
June 29: Figs from Thistles

1920
November 13: The Bean Stalk
December 18: To the not impossible him, Daphne, She is Overheard Singing

1921
February 26: To a poet that died young
August 6: City Trees, Prayer to Persephone, Travel, Assault

1922
June 3: Ballad of the Harp-weaver
October 14: Autumn Chant

1923
May 19: The Cairn, The Concert
June 9: Never May the Fruit Be Plucked, To a Dying Man, Renascence, portrait
July 7: Keen
October 13: From a Very Little Sphinx

1924
January 26: The Curse

1925
September 5: Not that it matters, not that my heart's cry
December 19: Armistice Day Parade

1926
January 16: The Pioneer

1927
March 19: Oh Caesar great wert thou and criticism and portrait.

1928
July 7: Dirge Without Music
October 13: Lethe
October 27: Moriturus, To a musician

1930
September 20: As men have loved their lovers in times past

1931
January 10: If in the years to come you should recall
July 18: Hearing your words and not a word among them

1934
February 3: portrait

Literary Review
June 16, 1923: Spring Song
October 4, 1924: portrait

Little Acorns, p. 86.

LITTLE ANTHOLOGY OF VERY SHORT POEMS FROM THE MAGAZINES OF 1921, A (appearance), p. 150.

Little, Brown & Company, p. 92.

Little Ghost, The—RENASCENCE AND OTHER POEMS; THE MELODY OF EARTH; POEMS; POEMS SELECTED FOR YOUNG PEOPLE; UNBOUND ANTHOLOGY.

Little Hill, The—SECOND APRIL; POEMS SELECTED FOR YOUNG PEOPLE.

Little Tavern, The—See: Tavern.

LITTLE TAVERN, THE (music), p. 155.

Little Theatre, The, St. Louis, p. 82.

LITTLE WORLD, 1914 AND AFTER, THE (criticism), p. 189.

[214]

Index

Index

Index

Index

Index

Index

Index

Index

Index

Index

Index

Index

Index

Index

Index

Index

She had a horror he would die at night—*Harpers*, May, 1923; THE HARP-WEAVER AND OTHER POEMS.

She had forgotten how the August night—*Harpers*, May, 1923; THE HARP-WEAVER AND OTHER POEMS.

She let them leave their jellies—*Harpers*, May, 1923; THE HARP-WEAVER AND OTHER POEMS.

Since I cannot persuade you from this mood—FATAL INTERVIEW.

Since of no creature living the last breath—*Delineator*, February, 1931; FATAL INTERVIEW.

So she came back into his house again—*Harpers*, May, 1923; THE HARP-WEAVER AND OTHER POEMS.

Sometimes when I am weary suddenly—*Reedy's Mirror*, May 13, 1920; THE HARP-WEAVER AND OTHER POEMS; BOOK OF SONNET SEQUENCES.

Sonnet to Gath—See: Country of Hunchbacks! Where the strong straight spine.

Sorrowful dreams remembered after waking—FATAL INTERVIEW.

Still will I harvest beauty where it grows—*Reedy's Mirror*, May 13, 1920; THE HARP-WEAVER AND OTHER POEMS; BOOK OF SONNET SEQUENCES.

Strange thing that I, by nature nothing prone—*Saturday Evening Post*, December 6, 1930; FATAL INTERVIEW.

Summer, be seen no more within this wood—FATAL INTERVIEW.

Sweeter was loss than silver coins to spend—WINE FROM THESE GRAPES.

Sweet love, sweet thorn, when lightly to my heart—*New Republic*, March 18, 1931; FATAL INTERVIEW.

Sweet sounds, oh beautiful music, do not cease!—*New Republic*, June 13, 1928; THE BUCK IN THE SNOW.

Tenderly, in those times, as though she fed—*Harpers*, May, 1923; THE HARP-WEAVER AND OTHER POEMS.

That Love at length should find—THE HARP-WEAVER AND OTHER POEMS.

The broken dike, the levee washed away—WINE FROM THESE GRAPES.

The doctor asked her what she wanted done—*Harpers*, May, 1923; THE HARP-WEAVER AND OTHER POEMS.

The heart once broken is a heart no more—*Harpers*, April, 1931; FATAL INTERVIEW.

The last white sawdust on the floor was grown—*Harpers*, May, 1923; THE HARP-WEAVER AND OTHER POEMS.

The light comes back with Columbine; she brings—*Reedy's Mirror*, May 6, 1920; THE HARP-WEAVER AND OTHER POEMS; BOOK OF SONNET SEQUENCES.

Then cautiously she pushed the cellar door—*Harpers*, May, 1923; THE HARP-WEAVER AND OTHER POEMS.

There is a well into whose bottomless eye—*Delineator*, January, 1931; FATAL INTERVIEW.

There was upon the sill a pencil mark—*Harpers*, May, 1923; THE HARP-WEAVER AND OTHER POEMS.

The wagon stopped before the house—*Harpers*, May, 1923; THE HARP-WEAVER AND OTHER POEMS.

The white bark writhed and sputtered like a fish—*Harpers*, May, 1923; THE HARP-WEAVER AND OTHER POEMS.

Think not, nor for a moment let your mind—FATAL INTERVIEW.

This beast that rends me in the

Index

Index

Yet in an hour to come, disdainful dust—FATAL INTERVIEW.

You loved me not at all, but let it go—FATAL INTERVIEW.

Your face is like a chamber where a king—THE HARP-WEAVER AND OTHER POEMS; POEMS SELECTED FOR YOUNG PEOPLE.

You say: "Since life is cruel enough at best"—FATAL INTERVIEW.

T

Taggard, Genevieve, pp. 151, 190, 191.

TAKING A LITERARY PULSE, p. 188.

Tate, Allen, pp. 189, 191.

Tavern—*Poetry*, August, 1917; *Literary Digest*, September 8, 1917; RENASCENCE AND OTHER POEMS; STAR POINTS; POEMS; THE LITTLE TAVERN (music); POEMS SELECTED FOR YOUNG PEOPLE.

Taylor, Deems, pp. 110, 111, 112, 116, 136.

Tea for the Muse—Boyd—*Vanity Fair*, January, 1922; DISTRESSING DIALOGUES.

Tea o' Herbs—See: A TREE WITH A BIRD IN IT.

Tenderly, in those times, as though she fed (sonnet) —*Harpers*, May, 1923; THE HARP-WEAVER AND OTHER POEMS.

TEN MODERN POETS (criticism), p. 189.

That Love at length should find me out and bring (sonnet) —THE HARP-WEAVER AND OTHER POEMS.

"That's not the point," Carl said; the point is not—*Harpers*, November, 1935; CONVERSATION AT MIDNIGHT.

That which is Love's—*Ainslee's*, May, 1919.

The broken dike, the levee washed away (sonnet) —*St. Louis Post-Dispatch*, December 9, 1928; WINE FROM THESE GRAPES.

The doctor asked her what she wanted done (sonnet) —*Harpers*, May, 1923; THE HARP-WEAVER AND OTHER POEMS.

The heart once broken is a heart no more (sonnet) —*Harpers*, April, 1931; FATAL INTERVIEW.

The last white sawdust on the floor was grown (sonnet) —*Harpers*, May, 1923; THE HARP-WEAVER AND OTHER POEMS.

The light comes back with Columbine; she brings (sonnet) —*Reedy's Mirror*, May 6, 1920; THE HARP-WEAVER AND OTHER POEMS; BOOK OF SONNET SEQUENCES.

Then cautiously she pushed the cellar door (sonnet) —*Harpers*, May, 1923; THE HARP-WEAVER AND OTHER POEMS.

There at dusk I found you—*Delineator*, September, 1928; THE BUCK IN THE SNOW.

There is a well into whose bottomless eye (sonnet) —*Delineator*, January, 1931; FATAL INTERVIEW.

There was upon the sill a pencil mark (sonnet) —*Harpers*, May, 1923; THE HARP-WEAVER AND OTHER POEMS.

The wagon stopped before the house (sonnet) —*Harpers*, May, 1923; THE HARP-WEAVER AND OTHER POEMS.

The white bark writhed and sputtered like a fish (sonnet) —*Harpers*, May, 1923; THE HARP-WEAVER AND OTHER POEMS.

Think not, nor for a moment let your mind (sonnet) —FATAL INTERVIEW.

This beast that rends me in the sight of all (sonnet) —*Harpers*, December, 1930; FATAL INTERVIEW.

This door you might not open and

Index

Index

Index

Index

[236]

Index

Bibliography

Date   , 19

TITLE:

Title-page:

Appearance of title-page:

Collation: Pp. $+$, consisting of

Size: $\times$ Bound in

Front cover:

Back bone:

Back cover:

Edges:

Published   , 19   . Copies deposited   , 19

The first edition may be identified by

Edna St. Vincent Millay

Date   , 19

TITLE:

Title-page:

Appearance of title-page:

Collation: Pp.   +   , consisting of

Size: ✕   Bound in

Front cover:

Back bone:

Back cover:

Edges:

Published   , 19   . Copies deposited   , 19

The first edition may be identified by

[240]

Bibliography

Date   , 19

TITLE:

Title-page:

Appearance of title-page:

Collation: Pp.   +   , consisting of

Size: ×   Bound in

Front cover:

Back bone:

Back cover:

Edges:

Published   , 19   . Copies deposited   , 19

The first edition may be identified by

[241]

Edna St. Vincent Millay

Date   , 19

TITLE:

Title-page:

Appearance of title-page:

Collation: Pp.   +   , consisting of

Size: ✕   Bound in

Front cover:

Back bone:

Back cover:

Edges:

Published   , 19   . Copies deposited   , 19

The first edition may be identified by

Bibliography

Date   , 19

TITLE:

Title-page:

Appearance of title-page:

Collation: Pp.   +   , consisting of

Size: ✕   Bound in

Front cover:

Back bone:

Back cover:

Edges:

Published   , 19   . Copies deposited   , 19

The first edition may be identified by

Edna St. Vincent Millay

Date   , 19

TITLE:

Title-page:

Appearance of title-page:

Collation: Pp.   +   , consisting of

Size: ×   Bound in

Front cover:

Back bone:

Back cover:

Edges:

Published   , 19   . Copies deposited   , 19

The first edition may be identified by

Bibliography

Date   , 19

TITLE:

Title-page:

Appearance of title-page:

Collation: Pp.   +   , consisting of

Size: ✕   Bound in

Front cover:

Back bone:

Back cover:

Edges:

Published   , 19   . Copies deposited   , 19

The first edition may be identified by

Edna St. Vincent Millay

Date   , 19

TITLE:

Title-page:

Appearance of title-page:

Collation: Pp.   +   , consisting of

Size: ✕   Bound in

Front cover:

Back bone:

Back cover:

Edges:

Published   19   . Copies deposited   , 19

The first edition may be identified by

[246]

Bibliography

Date   , 19

Title:

Title-page:

Appearance of title-page:

Collation: Pp.   +   , consisting of

Size: ×   Bound in

Front cover:

Back bone:

Back cover:

Edges:

Published   , 19   . Copies deposited   , 19

The first edition may be identified by

[247]

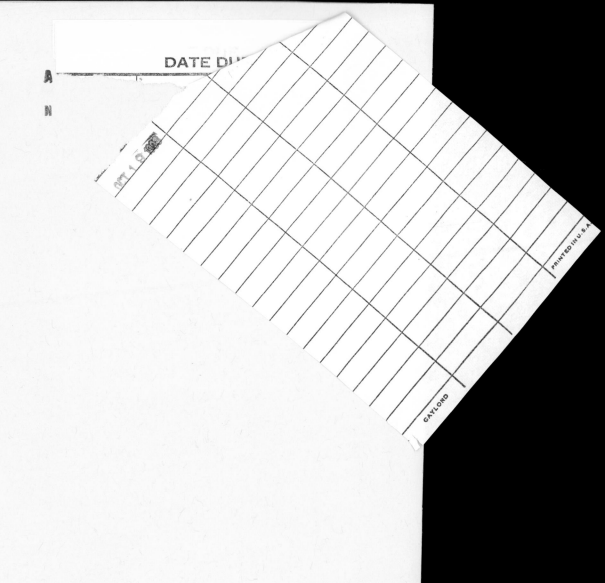